Benjamin Franklin DeCosta

The pre-Columbian Discovery of America by the Northmen

Illustrated by Translations from the Icelandic Sagas

Benjamin Franklin DeCosta

The pre-Columbian Discovery of America by the Northmen
Illustrated by Translations from the Icelandic Sagas

ISBN/EAN: 9783744767187

Printed in Europe, USA, Canada, Australia, Japan

Cover: Foto ©ninafisch / pixelio.de

More available books at **www.hansebooks.com**

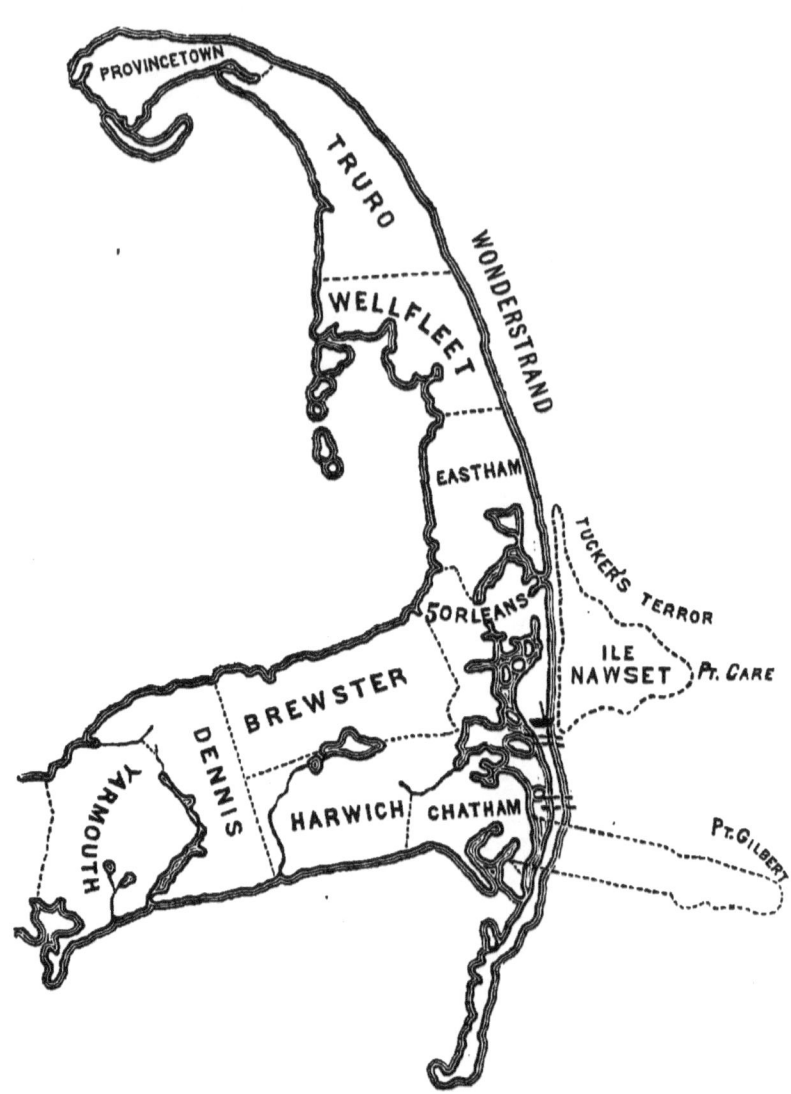

A MAP OF CAPE COD AS IT APPEARED AT THE BEGINNING OF THE 17TH CENTURY.

See page 30.

THE PRE-COLUMBIAN DISCOVERY OF AMERICA

BY

THE NORTHMEN,

ILLUSTRATED BY

Translations from the Icelandic Sagas,

EDITED WITH

NOTES AND A GENERAL INTRODUCTION,

BY

B. F. DE COSTA.

ALBANY:
JOEL MUNSELL.
1868.

PREFACE.

The aim of the present work is to place within the reach of the English reading historical student every portion of the Icelandic Sagas essentially relating to the Pre-Columbian Discovery of America by the Northmen. These Sagas are left, in the main, to tell their own story; though, with the necessary introductions, notes have been added, either to remove misconceptions, to give information in regard to persons and places, or to show the identity of localities described.

So long ago as the year 1838, a distinguished writer in the *North American Review*, in closing a valuable and appreciative article on the Sagas relating to America, said : "We trust that some zealous student of these subjects will be immediately found, who will put the Icelandic authorities into an English dress, and prepare them, with proper literary apparatus, for the perusal of the general reader."

Nevertheless, no one in this country has really undertaken the task until now; for the dialogues of Joshua Toulmin Smith, however valuable they may have proved at the date of their publication, can by no means be regarded as constituting the strict historical work contemplated. The English treatise by Beamish was conceived in the right spirit; but, while encumbered with much irrelevant matter, it did not complete the subject, and, together with Smith's work, long since went out of print. Several of the brief Narratives are also given by Laing, buried in the appendix of his valuable translation of the *Heimskringla;* but the labors of these authors are not now available, and, if combined, would not meet the present want. The author has therefore improved a favorable occasion to present what may, perhaps, be regarded as an exposition of the whole question. In doing so he has freely made use of such material from the above mentioned writers as he considered valuable for the purpose. The brief translations of Laing, being well done, have been given entire, with the exception that particular expressions have been improved upon; but such portions of the unsatisfactory and not altogether ingenuous work of Smith as have been used have been somewhat thoroughly recast. A better use could have been made of Beamish's work, if the author had succeeded in obtaining a copy before he was on the point of closing up his work.

No critical knowledge of the Icelandic tongue is claimed by the author, yet he hopes that the text of the Sagas has not here been misinterpreted, or left obscure, especially as the Sagas relating to the Pre-Columbian voyages are given in Professors Rafn's work on the antiquities of America, accompanied by versions in Latin and Danish. In everything relating to the latter tongue, the author has had the invaluable assistance and advice of one who has spoken it from childhood.

The grammatical structure of the Icelandic is simple, and the aim has been throughout to maintain this simplicity in the translations, so far as the genius of our own tongue would permit. This work being strictly historical, both in spirit and design, the poetical extracts which occur here and there are translated as literally as possible, without any attempt to garnish them with metre and rhyme. Nevertheless versions in rhyme, by other hands, are sometimes given in the notes.

It will be seen that the author differs on some points from Professor Rafn; yet it is believed that if he could have gone over the subject again, studying it on the ground, and amid the scenes in which so many of the exploits of the Northmen were performed, he would have modified his views on some points.

On the other hand, the author has sought to strengthen several of the conclusions of that noble and laborious investigator, and particularly by bringing out more fully the truthfulness of the Icelandic descriptions of the coast of Cape Cod, which centuries ago presented an aspect that it does not now possess.

And let us remember that in vindicating the Northmen we honor those who not only give us the first knowledge possessed of the American continent, but to whom we are indebted for much beside that we esteem valuable. For we fable in a great measure when we speak of our "Saxon inheritance." It is rather from the Northmen that we have derived our vital energy, our freedom of thought, and, in a measure, that we do not yet suspect, our strength of speech. Yet, happily, the people are fast becoming conscious of their indebtedness; so that it is to be hoped that the time is not far distant when the Northmen may be recognized in their right, social, political and literary characters, and at the same time, as navigators, assume their true position in the Pre-Columbian Discovery of America.

STUYVESANT PARK,
    NEW YORK, 1868.

CONTENTS.

I. Preface.

II. General Introduction.—Historic Fancies; The Sea of Darkness; Juba's Expedition; Traditions; The Northmen; The Colonization of Iceland; Settlement of Greenland; Organization of the Church; Monuments and Ruins; Explorations in Greenland; The Decline of Greenland; Lost Greenland Found; The Character and Achievments of the Northmen; The Ships of the Northmen; The Literature of Iceland; The Manuscripts; The Truthfulness of the Narratives; The Absence of Monuments and Remains in Vinland.

III. Gunnbiorn and his Rocks.

IV. Eric the Red's voyages to Greenland and settlement, A.D. 983-986.

V. Biarne Heriulfsson's voyage to the coast of America, A.D. 986.

VI. Leif Ericson's voyage to Vinland, - - - - A.D. 1000-1001.

VII. Thorvald Ericson's voyage to Vinland, - - A.D. 1002.

VIII. Thorstein Ericson's attempt to Seek Vinland, - A.D. 1005.

IX. Thorfinn Karlsefne's settlement in Vinland, - A.D. 1006-1009.

X. Freydis's voyage and settlement in Vinland, - - A.D. 1010-1012.

MINOR NARRATIVES.

I. Are Marson's Sojourn in Hvitramannaland, - - - A.D. 983.

II. Voyage of Biorn Asbrandson, - - - - - A.D. 999.

III. Gudleif Gudlangson's voyage, - - - - - A.D. 1027.

IV. Allusions to Voyages found in Ancient Manuscripts.

V. Geographical Fragments.

GENERAL INTRODUCTION.

PRE-COLUMBIAN DISCOVERY.

GENERAL INTRODUCTION.

HISTORIC FANCIES.

Before the plains of Europe, or even the peaks of Choumalarie, rose above the primeval seas, the Continent of America emerged from the watery waste that encircled the whole globe, and became the scene of animate life. The so-called New World is in reality the Old, and bears abundant proofs of hoary age. But at what period it became the abode of man we are unable even to conjecture. Down to the close of the tenth century of the Christian era it had no written history. Traces of a rude civilization that suggest a high antiquity are by no means wanting. Monuments and mounds remain that point to periods the contemplation of which would cause Chronos himself to grow giddy; yet among all these great and often impressive memorials there is no monument, inscription, or sculptured frieze, that solves the mystery of their origin. Tradition itself is dumb, and the theme chiefly kindles when brought within the realm of imagination. We can only infer that age after age nations and tribes continued to rise to greatness and then fall into decline, and that barbarism and a rude culture held alternate sway.

Nevertheless, men have enjoyed no small degree of satisfaction in conjuring up theories to explain the origin of the early races on the Western Continent. What a charm lingers around the supposed trans-Atlantic voyages of the hardy Phenician, the luxurious sailors of Tyre, and, later, of the bold Basque. What stories might the lost picture-records of Mexico and the chronicles of Dieppe tell. Now we are presented with the splendid view of great fleets, the remnant of some conquered race, bearing across the ocean to re-create in new and unknown lands the cities and monuments they were forever leaving behind;[1] and now it is simply the story of some storm-tossed mariner who blindly drives across to the western strand, and lays the foundation of empire. Again it is the devotee of mammon, in search of gainful traffic or golden fleece. How romantic is the picture of his little solitary bark setting out in the days of Roman greatness, or in the splendid age of Charlemagne, sailing trustingly away between the Pillars of Hercules, and tossing towards the Isles of the Blessed and the Fountains of Eternal Youth. In time the *Ultima Thule* of the known world is passed, and favoring gales bear the merchant-sailor to new and wondrous lands. We see him coasting the unknown shores passing from cape to cape, and from bay to inlet, gazing upon the marvels of the New World, trafficing with the bronzed Indian, bartering curious wares for barbaric gold; and then shaping his course again for the markets of the distant East to pour strange tales into incredulous ears. Still this may not be all fancy.

THE SEA OF DARKNESS.

In early times the Atlantic ocean, like all things without known bounds, was viewed by man with mixed feelings of fear and awe. It was called the Sea of Darkness. Yet, nevertheless, there were those who professed to have some knowledge of its extent, and of what lay beyond. The earliest reference to this sea is that by Theopompus, in the

---

[1] See Jones on *The Tyrian Period of America*.

fourth century before the Christian era, given in a fragment of Ælian,[1] where a vast island is described, lying far in the west, and peopled by strange races. To this we may add the reference of Plato[2] to the island called Atlantis, which lay west of the Pillars of Hercules, and which was estimated to be larger than Asia and Africa combined. Aristotle[3] also thought that many other lands existed beyond the Atlantic. Plato supposed that the Atlantis was sunk by an earthquake, and Crantor says that he found the same account related by the Priests of Sais three hundred years after the time of Solon, from whom the grandfather of Critias had his information. Plato says, that after the Atlantis disappeared navigation was rendered too difficult to be attempted by the slime which resulted from the sinking of the land. It is probable that he had in mind the immense fields of drifting sea-weed found in that locality, and which Humboldt estimates to cover a portion of the Atlantic ocean six times as large as all Germany.

It is thought that Homer[4] obtained the idea of his Elysium in the Western ocean from the voyages of the Phenicians, who, as is well known, sailed regularly to the British Islands. They are also supposed by some to have pushed their discoveries as far as the Western Continent. Cadiz, situated on the shore of Andalusia, was established by the Tyrians twelve centuries before the year of Christ; and when Cadiz, the ancient Gadir, was full five hundred years old, a Greek trader, Colæus, there bought rare merchandise, a long and severe gale having driven his ships beyond the Pillars of Hercules.

---

[1] *Var. Hist.*, lib. III, cap. xviii.
[2] See Plato's *Critias and Timæus*.
[3] *De Mundo*, cap. III. See *Prince Henry the Navigator*, chap. VII, by Major: London, 1868.
[4] *Odyssey*, book IV, l. 765.

THE PHENICIANS.

In the ninth century before the Christian Era, the Phenicians had established colonies on the western coast of Africa; and three hundred years later, according to Herodotus, Pharaoh Necho, son of Psammiticus, sent an expedition, manned by Phenician sailors, around the entire coast of Africa. Vivien de St. Martin fixes the date of this expedition at 570 before Christ. St. Martin, in his account of the voyage, improves slightly upon the views of Carl Müller, and is followed by Bougainville.[1] This voyage, performed by Hanno under the direction of Pharaoh, was inscribed in the Punic language in a Carthagenian temple, being afterwards translated into Greek, and was thus preserved.

That the Canary Islands were discovered and colonized by the Phenicians, there need be no doubt. Tradition had always located islands in that vicinity. Strabo speaks of the Islands of the Blessed, as lying not far from Mauritania, opposite Gadir or Cadiz. And he distinctly says, "That those who pointed out these things were *the Phenicians*, who, before the time of Homer, had possession of the best part of Africa and Spain."[2] And when we remember that the Phenicians sought to monopolize trade, and hold the knowledge of their commercial resorts a secret, it is not surprising that we should hear nothing more of the Fortunate Isles until about eighty-two years before Christ, when the Roman Sertorius met some Lusitanian sailors on the coast of Spain who had just returned from the Fortunate Isles. They are described as two delightful islands, separated by a narrow strait, distant

---

[1] See *Prince Henry the Navigator*, p. 90.
[2] Strabo. lib. III.—*Plutarch*.

from Africa five hundred leagues. Twenty years after the death of Sertorius, Statius Sebosus drew up a chart of a group of five islands, each mentioned by name, and which Pliny calls the Hesperides, including the Fortunate Isles. This mention of the Canaries was sixty-three years before Christ.

JUBA'S EXPEDITION.

When King Juba II returned to Mauritania, he sent an expedition to the Fortunate Isles. A fragment of the narratives of this expedition still survives in the works of Pliny. They are described as lying southwest, six hundred and twenty-five miles from Purpurariæ. To reach them from this place, they first sailed two hundred and fifty miles westward and then three hundred and seventy-five miles eastward. Pliny says: "The first is called Ombrios, and contains no traces of buildings. There is in it a pool in the midst of mountains, and trees like ferules, from which water may be pressed, which is bitter from the black kinds, but from the light kinds pleasant to drink. The second is called Junonia, and contains a small temple built entirely of stone. Near it is another smaller island having the same name. Then comes Capraria, which is full of large lizards. Within sight of these is Nivaria, so called from the snow and fogs with which it is always covered. Not far from Nivaria is Canaria, so called on account of the great number of large dogs therein, two of which were brought to King Juba. There were traces of buildings in these islands. All the islands abound in apples, and in birds of every kind, and in palms covered with dates, and in the pine nut. There is also plenty of fish. The papyrus grows there, and the silurus fish is found in the rivers."[1]

---

[1] Pliny's *Natural History*, lib. VI, cap. 37.

The author of *Prince Henry the Navigator*,[1] says that in Ombrios, we recognize the Pluvialia of Sebosus. Convallis of Sebosus, in Pliny, becomes Nivaria, the Peak of Teneriffe, which lifts itself up to the majestic height of nine thousand feet, its snow-capped pinnacle seeming to pierce the sky. Planaria is displaced by Canaria, which term first applied to the great central island, now gives the name to the whole group. Ombrios or Pluvialia, evidently means the island of Palma, which had "a pool in the midst of mountains," now represented by the crater of an extinct volcano. This the sailors of King Juba evidently saw. Major says: "The distance of this island [Palma] from Fuerteventura, agrees with that of the two hundred and fifty miles indicated by Juba's navigators as existing between Ombrios and the Purpurariæ. It has already been seen that the latter agree with Lancerote and Fuerteventura, in respect of their distance from the continent and from each other, as described by Plutarch. That the Purpurariæ are not, as M. Bory de St. Vincent supposed, the Madeira group, is not only shown by the want of inhabitants in the latter, but by the orchil, which supplies the purple dye, being derived from and sought for especially from the Canaries, and not from the Madeira group, although it is to be found there. Junonia," he continues, "the nearest to Ombrios, will be Gomera. It may be presumed that the temple found therein, was, like the island, dedicated to Juno. Capraria, which implies the island of goats, agrees correctly with the island of Ferro, . . . for these animals were found there in large numbers when the island was invaded by Jean de Bethencourt, in 1402. But a yet more striking proof of the identity of this island with Capraria, is the account of the great number of lizards found therein. Bethencourt's

---

[1] See p. 137.

chaplains, describing their visit to the islands, in 1402, state : 'There are lizards in it as big as cats, but they are harmless, although very hideous to look at.'"[1]

We see, then, that the navigators of Juba visited the Canaries[2] at an early period, as Strabo testifies was the case with the Phenicians, who doubtless built the temple in the island of Junonia. And, for aught we know, early navigators may have passed over to the Western continent and laid the foundation of those strange nations whose monuments still remain. Both Phenician and Tyrian voyages to the Western Continent, have been warmly advocated; while Lord Kingsborough published his magnificent volumes on the Mexican Antiquities, to show that the Jews settled this continent at an early day.[3] And if it is true that all the tribes of the earth sprang from one central Asiatic family, it is more than likely that the original inhabitants of the American continent crossed the Atlantic, instead of piercing the frozen regions of the north, and coming in by the way of Behring Straits. From the Canaries to the coast of Florida, it is a short voyage, and the bold sailors of the Mediterranean, after

---

[1] *Prince Henry the Navigator*, p. 137.

[2] After this mention by Pliny, the Canaries, or Fortunate Isles, are lost sight of for a period of thirteen hundred years. In the reign of Edward III of England, at the beginning of the fourteenth century, one Robert Machin sailed from Bristol for France, carrying away a lady of rank, who had eloped with him, and was driven by a storm to the Canaries, where he landed, and thus rediscovered the lost Fortunate Isles. This fact is curiously established by Major, in the *Life of Prince Henry*, so that it can no longer be regarded as an idle tale (see pp. 66-77). In 1341, a voyage was also made to the Canaries, under the auspices of King Henry of Portugal. The report, so widely circulated by De Barros, that the islands were rediscovered by Prince Henry is therefore incorrect. His expedition reached Porto Santo and Madeira in 1418-20.

[3] He also speculates upon the probability of this continent having been visited by Christian missionaries. See vol. VI, p. 410.

touching at the Canaries, need only spread their sails before the steady-breathing monsoon, to find themselves wafted safely to the western shore.

TRADITIONS.

There was even a tradition that America was visited by St. Columba,[1] and also by the Apostle St. Thomas,[2] who penetrated even as far as Peru. This opinion is founded on the resemblance existing between certain rites and doctrines which *seem* to have been held in common by Christians and the early inhabitants of Mexico. The first Spanish missionaries were surprised to find the Mexicans bowing in adoration before the figure of the cross, and inferred that these people were of a Christian origin. Yet the inference has no special value, when we remember that Christianity is far less ancient than the symbol of the cross, which also existed among the Egyptians and other ancient people.

Claims have also been made for the Irish. Broughton brings forward a passage in which St. Patrick is represented as sending missionaries to the Isles of America.[3] Another claim has been urged of a more respectable character, which is supported by striking, though not conclusive allusions in the chronicles of the North, in which a distant land is spoken of as "Ireland the Great." The Irish, in the early times, might easily have passed over to the Western continent, for which voyage they undoubtedly had the facilities. And Professor Rafn, after alluding to the well known fact that the Northmen were preceded in Iceland by the Irish, says, that it is by no means

---

[1] Kingsborough's *Mexican Antiquities*, vol. VI, p. 285.

[2] Ibid., p. 332.

[3] *Monastikon Britannicum*, pp. 131-2-187-8. The fact that the word *America* is here used, seems quite sufficient to upset the legend.

improbable that the Irish should also have anticipated them in America. The Irish were a sea-faring people, and have been assigned a Phenician origin by Moore and others who have examined the subject.[1] If this is so, the tradition would appear to be some what strengthened. Even as early as the year 296, the Irish are said to have invaded Denmark with a large fleet. In 396, Niall made a descent upon the coast of Lancashire with a considerable navy, where he was met by the Roman, Stilicho, whose achievements were celebrated by Claudian in the days of the Roman occupation of England. At that period the Irish were in most respects in advance of the Northmen, not yet having fallen into decline, and quite as likely as any people then existing to brave the dangers of an ocean voyage.[2] The Icelandic documents, possibly referring to the Irish, will be given in their proper place, and in the meanwhile it need only to be added that the quotation given by Beamish from such an authority as the *Turkish Spy* will hardly tend to strengthen their claims, especially where its author, John Paul Marana, says that in Mexico "the British language is so prevalent," that "the very towns, bridges, beasts, birds,

---

[1] The Irish were early known as Scots, and O'Halloran derives the name from Scota, high priest of Phœnius, and ancestor of Milesouis.

    Me quoque vicins pereuntem gentibus, inquit,
    Munivit Stilicho. Totam cum Scotus Iernem,
    Movit et infesto spumavit remige Thetys.

    By him defended, when the neighboring hosts
    Of warlike nations spread along our coasts;
    When Scots came thundering from the Irish shores,
    And the wide ocean foamed with hostile oars.

[2] Speaking of Britain and Ireland, Tacitus says of the latter, that "the approaches and harbors are better known, by reason of commerce and the merchants."—*Vit. Agri.*, c. 24. The Irish, doubtless, mingled with the Carthagenians in mercantile transactions, and from them they not unlikely received the rites of Druidism.

rivers, hills, etc., are called by the British or Welch[1] names."[2] In truth, as the wish is so often father to the thought, it would be an easy task to find resemblance in the languages of the aborigines to almost any language that is spoken in our day.

But notwithstanding the *probabilities* of the case, we have no solid reason for accepting any of these alleged voyages as facts. Much labor has been given to the subject, yet the early history of the American continent is still veiled in mystery, and not until near the close of the tenth century of the present era can we point to a genuine trans-Atlantic voyage.

THE NORTHMEN.

The first voyage to America, of which we have any account, was performed by Northmen. But who were the Northmen?

The Northmen were the descendants of a race that in early times migrated from Asia and traveled towards the north, finally settling in what is now the kingdom of Denmark. From thence they overran Norway and Sweden, and afterwards colonized Iceland and Greenland. Their language was the old Danish (*Dönsk túnga*) once spoken all over the north,[3] but which is now preserved in Iceland alone, being called the Icelandic or old North,[4] upon

---

[1] As the tradition of a Welch voyage to America under Prince Madoc, relates to a period *following* the Icelandic voyages, the author does not deem it necessary to discuss the subject. This voyage by the son of Owen Gwyneth, is fixed for the year 1170, and is based on a Welch chronicle of no authority. See *Hackluyt*, vol. III, p. 1.

[2] *Turkish Spy*, vol. VIII, p. 159.

[3] See "Northmen in Iceland," *Sociétà des Antiquaires du Nord, Seance du 14 Mai*, 1859, pp. 12–14.

[4] It is sometimes, though improperly, called the *Norse*.

which is founded the modern Swedish, Danish and Norse or Norwegian.

After the Northmen had pushed on from Denmark to Norway, the condition of public affairs gradually became such that a large portion of the better classes found their life intolerable. In the reign of Harold Harfagr (the Fair-haired), an attempt was made by the king to deprive the petty jarls of their ancient udal or feudal rights, and to usurp all authority for the crown. To this the proud jarls would not submit; and, feeling themselves degraded in the eyes of their retainers, they resolved to leave those lands and homes which they could now hardly call their own. Whither, then, should they go?

THE COLONIZATION OF ICELAND.

In the cold north sea, a little below the arctic circle, lay a great island. As early as the year 860, it had been made known to the Northmen by a Dane of Swedish descent named Gardar, who called it Gardar's island, and four years later by the pirate Nadodd, who sailed thither in 864 and called it Snowland. Presenting in the main the form of an irregular elipse, this island occupies an area of about one hundred and thirty-seven square miles, affording the dull diversity of valleys without verdure and mountains without trees.[1] Desolation has there fixed its abode. It broods among the dells, and looks down upon the gloomy fiords. The country is threaded with streams and dotted with tarns, yet the geologist finds but little evidence in the structure of the earth to point to the action of water. On the other hand, every rock and hillside is covered with signs that prove their igneous

---

[1] In the time when the Irish monks occupied the island, it is said that it was "covered with woods between the mountains and the shores."

origin, and indicate that the entire island, at some distant period, has already seethed and bubbled in the fervent heat, in anticipation of the long promised *Palingenesia*. Even now the ground trembles in the throes of the earthquake, the Geyser spouts scalding water, and the plain belches mud; while the great jokull, clad in white robes of eternal snow — true priest of Ormuzd — brandishes aloft its volcanic torch, and threatens to be the incendiary of the sky.

The greater portion of the land forms the homestead of the reindeer and the fox, who share their domain with the occasional white bear that may float over from Greenland on some berg. Only two quadrupeds, the fox and the moose, are indigenous. Life is here purchased with a struggle. Indeed the neighboring ocean is more hospitable than the dry land, for of the thirty-four species of mammalia twenty-four find their food in the roaring main. The same is true of the feathered tribes, fifty-four out of ninety being water fowl. Here and there may be seen patches of meadow and a few sheep pastures and tracts of arable land warmed into fruitfulness by the brief summer's sun; yet, on the whole, so poor is the soil that man, like the lower orders, must eke out a scanty subsistence by resorting to the sea.

It was towards this land, which the settlers called *Iceland*, that the proud Norwegian jarl turned his eyes, and there he resolved to found a home.

The first settler was Ingolf. He approached the coast in the year 875, threw overboard his seat-posts,[1] and

---

[1] *Setstakkar.* These were wooden pillars carved with images usually of Thor and Odin. In selecting a place for a settlement these were flung overboard, and wherever they were thrown up on the beach, there the settlement was to be formed. Ingolf, the first Norse settler of Iceland, lost sight of the seat-posts after they were thrown into the water, and was obliged to live for the space of three years at Ingolfshofdi. In another

waited to see them touch the land. But in this he was disappointed, and those sacred columns, carved with the images of the gods, drifted away from sight. He nevertheless landed on a pleasant promontory at the south-eastern extremity of the island, and built his habitation on the spot which is called Ingolfshofdi to this day. Three years after, his servants found the seat-posts in the south-western part of the island, and hither, in obedience to what was held to be the expressed wish of the gods, he removed is household, laying the foundation of Reikiavik, the capital of this ice-bound isle. He was rapidly followed by others, and in a short time no inconsiderable population was gathered here.

But the first settlers did not find this barren country entirely destitute of human beings. Ari Frode,[1] than whom there is no higher anthority, says: "Then were here Christian people, whom the Northmen called papas, but they afterwards went away, because they would not be here among heathens; and left behind them Irish books,

---

case a settler did not find his posts for *twelve* years, nevertheless he changed his abode then. In Frithiof's Saga (American edition) chap. III, p. 18, we find the following allusion:

> "Through the whole length of the hall shone forth the table of oak wood,
> Brighter than steel, and polished; the pillars twain of the high seats
> Stood on each side thereof; two gods deep carved out of elm wood:
> Odin with glance of a king, and Frey with the sun on his forhead."

[1] Ari Hinn Frode, or the Wise. The chief compiler of the famous *Landnama Book*, which contains a full account of all the early settlers in Iceland. It is of the same character, though vastly superior to the English *Doomsday Book*, and is probably the most complete record of the kind ever made by any nation.

It contains the names of 3000 persons, and 1,400 places. It gives a correct account of the genealogies of the families, and brief notices of personal achievements. It was begun by Frode (born 1067, died 1148), and was continued by Kalstegg, Styrmer and Thordsen, and completed by Hauk Erlandson, Lagman, or Governor of Iceland, who died in the year 1334.

and bells, and croziers, from which it could be seen that they were Irishmen." He repeats substantially the same thing in the *Landanama Book*, the authority of which, no one acquainted with the subject, will question, adding that books and other relics were found in the island of Papey and Papyli, and that the circumstance is also mentioned in English books. The English writings referred to are those of the Venerable Bede. This is also stated in an edition of King Olaf Tryggvesson's Saga, made near the end of the fourteenth century.[1]

The monks or Culdees, who had come hither from Ireland and the Isles of Iona, to be alone with God, all took their departure on the arrival of the heathen followers of Odin and Thor, and the Northmen were thus left in undisputed possession of the soil. In about twenty years the island became quite thickly settled, though the tide of immigration continued to flow in strongly for fifty years, so that at the beginning of the tenth century Iceland possessed a population variously estimated from sixty to seventy thousand souls. But few undertook the voyage who were not able to buy their own vessels, in which they carried over their own cattle, and thralls, and household goods. So great was the number of people who left Norway at the outset that King Harold tried to prevent emigration by royal authority, though, as might have been predicted, his efforts were altogether in vain. Here, therefore, was formed a large community, taking the

---

[1] "Thus saith the holy priest Bede..... Therefore learned men think that it is Iceland which is called Thule..... But the holy priest Bede died DCCXXXV. years after the birth of our Lord Jesus Christ, more than a hundred years before Iceland was inhabited by the Northmen."—*Antiquitates Americanæ*, p. 202. .This extract is followed by the statement of Ari Frode, and shows that the Irish Christians retired to Iceland at a very early day. The Irish monk Dicuil also refers to this solitary island, which, about the year 795, was visited by some monks with whom he had conversed.

shape of an aristocratic republic, which framed its own laws, and for a long time maintained a genuine independence, in opposition to all the assumptions and threats of the Norwegian king.

THE SETTLEMENT OF GREENLAND.

But as time passed on, the people of Iceland felt a new impulse for colonization in strange lands, and the tide of emigration began to tend towards Greenland in the west. This was chiefly inaugurated by a man named Eric the Red, born in Norway in the year 935. On account of manslaughter, he was obliged to flee from Jardar and take up his abode in Iceland. The date of removal to Iceland is not given, though it is said that at the time the island was very generally inhabited. Here, however, he could not live in peace, and early in the year 982, he was again outlawed for manslaughter by the public Thnig, and condemned to banishment. He accordingly fitted out a ship, and announced his determination to go in search of the land lying in the ocean at the west, which, it was said, Gunnbiorn,[1] Ulf Kruge's son, saw, when, in the year 876, he was driven out to sea by a storm. Eric sailed westward and found land, where he remained and explored the country for three years. At the end of this period he returned to Iceland, giving the newly discovered land the name of Greenland,[2] in order, as he said, to attract settlers,

---

[1] All the information which we possess relating to the discovery by Gunnbiorn is given in the body of this work, in extracts from *Landanama-bok*.

[2] Claudius Christophessen, the author of some Danish verses relating to the history of Greenland, supposes that Greenland was discovered in the year 770, though he gave no real reason for his belief. *M. Peyrere* also tells us of a Papal Bull, issued in 835, by Gregory IV, which refers to the conversion of the Icelanders and Greenlanders. Yet this is beyond question

who would be favorably impressed by so pleasing a name.

The summer after his return to Iceland, he sailed once more for Greenland, taking with him a fleet of thirty-five ships, only fourteen of which reached their destination, the rest being either driven back or lost. This event took place, as the Saga says, fifteen winters[1] before the introduction of Christianity into Iceland, which we know was accomplished in the year A. D. 1000. The date of Eric's second voyage must therefore be set down at 985.[2] .

But, before proceeding to the next step in Icelandic adventure, it will be necessary to give a brief sketch of the progress of the Greenland colony, together with a relation of the circumstances which led to its final extinction.

THE PROGRESS OF THE GREENLAND COLONIES.

There is but little continuity in the history of the Icelandic occupation of Greenland. We have already seen that the second voyage of Eric the Red took place in the year 985. Colonists appear to have followed him in considerable numbers, and the best portions of the land were soon appropriated by the principal men, who gave the chief bays and capes names that indicated the occupants, following the example of Eric, who dwelt in Brattahlid, in Ericsfiord.

In the year 999, Leif, son of Eric, sailed out to Norway and passed the winter at the court of King Olaf Tryggvesson, where he accepted the Christian faith, which was then being zealously propagated by the king. He was

---

a fraud. Gunnbiorn was undoubtedly the first to gain a glimpse of Greenland.

[1] The Northmen reckoned by *winters*.

[2] See the Saga of Eric the Red.

accordingly baptized, and when the spring returned the king requested him to undertake the introduction of Christianity in Greenland, urging the consideration that no man was better qualified for the task. Accordingly he set sail from Norway, with a priest and several members of the religious order, arriving at Brattahlid, in Greenland, without any accident.[1] His pagan father was incensed by the bringing in of the Christian priest, which act he regarded as pregnant with evil; yet, after some persuasion on the part of Leif, he renounced heathenism and nominally accepted Christianity, being baptized by the priest. His wife Thorhild made less opposition, and appears to have received the new faith with much willingness. One of her first acts was to build a church, which was known far and wide as Thorhild's church.[2] These examples appear to have been very generally followed, and Christianity was adopted in both Iceland and Greenland at about the same period,[3] though its acceptance did not immediately produce any very radical change in the spiritual life of the people. In course of time a number of churches were built, the ruins of which remain down to our own day.

In the year 1003, the Greenlanders became tributary to Norway. The principal settlement was formed on the western coast, and what was known as the eastern district, did not extend farther than the southern extremity towards

---

[1] The statement, found in several places, that he discovered Vinland while on his way to Greenland, is incorrect. The full account of his voyages shows that his Vinland voyage was an entirely separate thing.

[2] The author designs shortly to give some full account of the early Christianity on the Western Continent in a separate work, now well advanced towards completion. It will include both the *Pre* and *Post*-Columbian eras.

[3] Gissur the White and Hialte, went on the same errand to Iceland in the year 1000, when the new religion was formally adopted at the public Thnig.

Cape Farewell. For a long time it was supposed that the east district was located on the eastern coast of Greenland; but the researches of Captain Graah, whose expedition went out under the auspices of the Danish government, proved very conclusively that no settlement ever existed on the eastern shore, which for centuries has remained blocked up by vast accumulations of ice that floated down from the arctic seas. In early times, as we are informed by the Sagas, the eastern coast was more accessible, yet the western shores were so superior in their attractions that the colonist fixed his habitation there. The site of the eastern settlement is that included in the modern district of Julian's Hope, now occupied by a Danish colony. The western settlement is represented by the habitation of Frederikshab, Godthaab, Sukkertoppen and Holsteinborg.

THE ORGANIZATION OF THE CHURCH.

In process of time the Christians in Greenland multiplied to such an extent, both by conversions and by the immigration from Iceland, that it was found necessary, in the beginning of the twelfth century to take some measures for the better government of the church, especially as they could not hope much for regular visits from the bishops of Iceland. They therefore resolved to make an effort to secure a bishop of their own. Eric Gnupson, of Iceland, was selected for the office, and proceeded to Greenland about the year 1112, without being regularly consecrated. He returned to Iceland in 1120, and afterwards went to Denmark, where he was consecrated in Lund, by Archbishop Adzer. Yet he probably never returned to his duties in Greenland, but soon after resigned that bishopric and accepted another,[1] thus leaving Greenland without a spiritual director.

In the year 1123, Sokke, one of the principal men of Greenland, assembled the people and represented to them that both the welfare of the Christian faith and their own honor demanded that they should follow the example of other nations and maintain a bishop. To this view they gave their unanimous approval; and Einar, son of Sokke, was appointed a delegate to the court of King Sigurd, of Norway. He carried a present of ivory and fur, and a petition for the appointment of a bishop. His mission was successful, and in the year 1126 Arnald, the successor of Eric,[2] came into Greenland, and set up the Episcopal seat at Gardar.[3] Torfæus and Baron Holberg,[4] give a list of seventeen bishops who ruled in Greenland, ending with Andrew. The latter was consecrated and went thither in 1408, being never heard of afterwards.

The history of Old Greenland is found in the *Ecclesiastical Annals*, and consists of a mere skeleton of facts. As in Iceland and Norway there was no end of broils and bloodshed. A very considerable trade was evidently carried on between that country and Norway, which is the case at the present time with Denmark. As the land afforded no materials for ships, they depended in a great measure upon others for communication with the mother countries, which finally proved disastrous.

---

[1] It will be seen hereafter that he went and established himself in Vinland.

[2] See *Memoires des Antiquaires du Nord*, p. 383.

[3] The location of Gardar is now uncertain. At one time it was supposed to have been situated on the eastern coast; but since it became so clear that the east coast was never inhabited, that view has been abandoned, though the name appears in old maps.

[4] See Crantz's *Greenland*, vol. I, p. 252.

MONUMENTS AND RUINS.

Their villages and farms were numerous. Together they probably numbered several hundred, the ruins now left being both abundant and extensive. Near Igaliko, which is supposed to be the same as the ancient Einarsfiord, are the ruins of a church, probably the cathedral of Gardar. It is called the Kakortok church. It was of simple but massive architecture, and the material was taken from the neighboring cliffs. The stone is rough hewn, and but few signs of mortar are visible. It is fifty-one feet long and twenty-five wide. The north and south walls are over four feet thick, while the end walls are still more massive.

Nor are other monuments wanting. At Igalikko, nine miles from Julian's Hope, a Greenlander being one day employed in obtaining stones to repair his house, found among a pile of fragments a smooth stone that bore, what seemed to him, written characters. He mentioned the circumstance to Mr. Mathieson, the colonial director at Julian's Hope, who inferred that it must be a runic stone. He was so fortunate as to find it afterwards, and he accordingly sent it to Copenhagen, where it arrived in the year 1830. The runes, which were perfectly distinct, showed that it was a tombstone. The inscription was translated as follows:

"VIGDIS MARS DAUGHTER RESTS HERE.
MAY GOD GLADDEN HER SOUL."

Another found in 1831, by the Rev. Mr. De Fries, principal of the Moravian Mission, bore the following inscription in the runic letter:

"HERE RESTS HROAR KOLGRIMSSON."

This stone, now in the museum at Copenhagen, was found built into the wall over the entrance of a Greenland house, having been taken for that purpose from a heap of ruins, about two miles north of Friederichsthal. This stone is more than three feet long, being eighteen inches wide in the narrowest part, and about five inches thick. It bears every sign of a high antiquity.

But one of the most interesting remains which prove the Icelandic occupation of Greenland is the runic stone found by Parry, in 1824, in the island of Kingiktorsoak, lying in 72° 55′ N. and 56° 51′ W. It contained a somewhat lengthy inscription, and copies of it were sent to three of the first scholars of the age, Finn Magnusson, Professor Rask, and Dr. Bryniulfson, who, without consultation, at once arrived at the same conclusion and united in giving the following translation:

"ERLING SIGHVATSON AND BIORN THORDARSON AND EINDRID ODDSON, ON SATURDAY BEFORE ASCENSION WEEK, RAISED THESE MARKS AND CLEARED GROUND. 1135.[1]

The Icelandic colonists in Greenland do not appear to have been confined to a small portion of territory. We find considerable relating to this subject in the chronicle attributed to Ivar Bert,[2] the steward of one of the bishops of Greenland; yet, though used extensively by Torfæus, modern researches in this country prove that it is in some respects faulty. In this chronicle, as in the Sagas, the

---

[1] These inscriptions are all in fair runic letters, about which there can be no mistake, and are totally unlike the imaginary runes, among which we may finally feel obliged to class those of the Dighton rock.

[2] See Egede's *Greenland*, p. xxv; Crantz's *Greenland*, vol. I, pp. 247–8; Purchas, *His Pilgrimes*, vol. III, p. 518; *Antiquitates Americanæ*, p. 300.

colonists are spoken of as possessing horses, sheep and oxen; and their churches and religious houses appear to have been well supported.

EXPLORATIONS IN GREENLAND.

Much was done, it appears, in the way of exploring the extreme northern portions of the country known as *Nordrsetur*. In the year 1266, a voyage was made under the auspices of some of the priests, and the adventurers penetrated north of Lancaster sound, reaching about the same latitude that was attained by Parry in 1827. This expedition was of sufficient importance to justify some notice of it here. The account is found in *Antiquitates Americanæ* (p. 269), and it sets out with the statement that the narrative of the expedition was sent by Haldor, a priest, to Arnald, the chaplain of King Magnus in Norway. They sailed out of Kroksfiardarheidi in an open boat, and met with southerly winds and thick weather, which forced them to let the boat drive before the wind. When the weather cleared, they saw a number of islands, together with whales and seals and bears. They made their way into the most distant portion of the sea, and saw glaciers south of them as far as the eye could reach. They also saw indications of the natives, who were called Skrællings, but did not land, on account of the number of the bears. They therefore put about, and laid their course southward for nearly three days, finding more islands, with traces of the natives. They saw a mountain which they call Snæfell, and on St. James day, July 25, they had a severe weather, being obliged to row much and very hard. It froze during the night in that region, but the sun was above the horizon both day and night. When the sun was on the southern meridian, and a man lay down crosswise in a six-oared boat, the shadow of the gunwale towards the sun would reach as far as his feet, which, of course, indicates that the sun was very low. Afterwards they all returned in safety to Gardar.[1] Rafn fixes the position of the point attained by the expedition in the parallel of 75° 46′. Such an achievement at that day indicates a degree of boldness quite surprising.

THE DECLINE OF GREENLAND.

Of the reality and importance of the Greenland colony there exists no doubt, notwithstanding the records are so meagre and fragmentary.[2] It maintained its connection with the mother countries for a period of no less than four hundred years; yet it finally disappeared and was almost forgotten.

The causes which led to the suspension of communication were doubtless various, though it is difficult to account for the utter extinction of the colony, which does not appear ever to have been in much danger from the Skrællings. On one occasion, in 1349 or later, the natives attacked the western settlement, it is said, and killed eighteen Greenlanders of Icelandic lineage, carrying away two boys captives.

We hear from the eastern colony as late as the middle of the fifteenth century. Trade was carried on with Denmark until nearly the end of the fourteenth century, although the voyages were not regular. The last bishop, Andreas, was sent out in 1406, and Professor Finn Magnussen has established the fact that he officiated in the cathedral at Gardar in 1409.[3]

---

[1] *Antiquitates Americanæ*, p. xxxix.

[2] For the account of the manuscripts upon which our knowledge of Greenland is founded, see *Antiquitates Americanæ*, p. 255.

[3] In that year parties are known to have contracted marriage at Gardar, from whom Finn Magnussen and other distinguished men owe their descent.

From this time the trade between Norway and Greenland appears to have been given up, though Wormius told Peyrere of his having read in a Danish manuscript that down to the year 1484 there was a company of more than forty sailors at Bergen, in Norway, who still traded with Greenland.[1] But as the revenue at that time belonged to Queen Margaret of Denmark, no one could go to Greenland without the royal permission. One company of sailors who were driven upon the Greenland coast, came near suffering the penalty of the law on their return. Crantz[2] says, that "about the year 1530, Bishop Amund of Skalholt in Iceland is said to have been driven by a storm, on his return from Norway, so near the coast of Greenland by Heriulfness, that he could see the people driving in their cattle. But he did not land, because just then a good wind arose, which carried the ship the same night to Iceland. The Icelander, Biærnvon Skardfa, who relates this, also says further, that a Hamburgh mariner, Jon Greenlander by name, was driven three times on the Greenland island, where he saw such fisher's huts for drying fish as they have in Iceland, but saw no men; further, that pieces of shattered boats, nay, in the year 1625, an entire boat, fastened together with sinews and wooden pegs, and pitched with seal blubber, have been driven ashore at Iceland from time to time; and since then they found once an oar with a sentence written in Runic letters : ' *Oft var ek dasa, dur elk drothik,*' that is, ' Oft was I tired when I drew thee.' "[3]

---

[1] Egede's *Greenland*, p. xlvii.
[2] Ibid., xlviii.
[3] Crantz's *Greenland*, vol. I, p. 264.

LOST GREENLAND FOUND.

But, whatever may be the value of the preceding extract, it is clear that Greenland was never wholly forgotten. The first person who proposed to reopen communication was Eric Walkendorf, Archbishop of Drontheim, who familiarized himself with the subject, and made every preparation necessary in order to reestablish the colony; but, having fallen under the displeasure of King Christian II, he left the country and went to Rome, where he died in the year 1521. Thus his plans came to nothing.[1] Christian III abrogated the decree of Queen Margaret, prohibiting trade with Greenland without the royal permission, and encouraged voyages by fitting out a vessel to search for Greenland, which, however, was not found. In 1578, Frederic II sent out Magnus Henningsen. He came in sight of the land, but does not appear to have had the courage to proceed further. Crantz, in his work on Greenland, gives an account of a number of voyages undertaken to the coast, but says that "at last Greenland was so buried in oblivion that one hardly would believe that such a land as Greenland was inhabited by Christian Norwegians."[2]

It remained, therefore, for Hans Egede,[3] in 1721, to reopen communication, and demonstrate the reality of the previous occupation. Columbus himself did not meet with greater trials and mortification than did this good man for the space of eleven years, during which period he labored to persuade the authorities to undertake the rediscovery. But his faith and zeal finally overcame all

---

[1] Crantz's *Greenland*, p. 274.
[2] Ibid., p. 279.
[3] Hans Egede was a clergyman in priest's orders, and minister of the congregation at Vogen in the northern part of Norway, where he was highly esteemed and beloved. He spent fifteen years as a missionary in Greenland, and died at Copenhagen, 1758.

hostility and ridicule, and on the second day of May, 1721, he went on board the Hope, with his wife and four young children, and landed at Ball's river in Greenland on the third of the following month. Here he spent the best portion of his life in teaching the natives Christianity, which had been first introduced seven centuries before, and in making those explorations the results of which filled the mind of Europe with surprise, and afforded a confirmation of the truthfulness of the Icelandic Sagas.

THE CHARACTER AND ACHIEVEMENTS OF THE NORTHMEN.

Let us now return to the consideration of the Icelandic voyages to the American Continent, though not without first seeking a better acquaintance with the men by whom they were performed.

We have already seen that the Northmen were a people of no inferior attainments. Indeed, they constituted the most enterprising portion of the race, and, on general principles, we should therefore view them as fitted even above all the men of their time for the important work of exploration beyond the seas. They had made themselves known in every part of the civilized world [1] by their daring as soldiers and navigators. Straying away into the distant east from whence they originally came, we see them laying the foundation of the Russian empire, swinging their battle-axes in the streets of Constantinople, carving their mystic runes upon the Lions of the Areopagus, and filling the heart of even the great Charlemagne with dismay. Says Dasent, when summing up their achievements: "In Byzantium they are the leaders of the Greek emperor's body guard, and the main support of his

---

[1] The motto on the sword of Roger Guiscard was:

"*Appulus et Calaber Siculus mihi Servit et Afer.*"

tottering throne. From France, led by Rollo, they tear
away her fairest province and found a long line of kings.
In Saxon England they are the bosom friends of such kings
as Athelstane, and the sworn foes of Ethelred the Unready.
In Danish England they are the foremost among the
thanes of Canute, Swein and Hardicanute, and keep down
the native population with an iron heel. In Norman
England," he continues, " the most serious opposition the
conqueror meets with is from the colonists of his own
race settled in Northumbria. He wastes their lands with
fire and sword, and drives them across the border, where
we still find their energy, their perseverance, and their
speech existing in the lowland Scotch. In Norway they
dive into the river with King Olaf Tryggvesson, the best
and strongest champion of his age, and hold him down
beneath the waves so long that the bystanders wonder
whether either king or Icelander will ever reappear on
the surface.[1] Some follow Saint Olaf in his crusades
against the old [pagan] faith.[2] Some are his obstinate
foes, and assist at his martyrdom. Many follow Harold
the Stern to England when he goes to get his ' seven feet '
of English earth, and almost to a man they get their
portion of the same soil, while their names grow bright
in song and story." And finally, "From Iceland as a
base, they push on to Greenland and colonize it: nay, they
discover America in those half-decked barks."[3]

THE SHIPS OF THE NORTHMEN.

The Northmen were excellent navigators. They were,
moreover, it has been claimed, the first to learn the art
of sailing on the wind. They had good sea-going vessels,

---

[1] See Laing's *Heimskringla*, vol. II, p. 450. This refers to his swimming match with Kiarten the Icelander, in which the king was beaten.

[2] See Saga of Saint (not king) Olaf.

[3] *Des Antiquaires du Nord*, 1859.

some of which were of large size. We have an account in the Saga of Olaf Tryggvesson of one that in some respects was remarkable. It is said that "the winter after King Olaf Tryggvesson came from Halogeland. He had a great ship built at Ledchammer,[1] which was larger than any ship in the country, and of which the beam-knees are still to be seen. The length of the keel that rested upon the grass was seventy-four ells. Thorberg Skafting was the man's name who was the master builder of the ship, but there were many others besides; some to fell the wood, some to shape it, some to make nails, some to carry timber, and all that was used was the best. The ship was both long and broad and high sided, and strongly timbered..... The ship was a dragon, built after the one that the king had captured in Halogaland, but it was far longer and more carefully put together in all her parts. The Long Serpent [her name] had thirty-four benches for rowers. The head and arched tail were both gilt, and the bulwarks were as high as in sea-going ships. This ship was the best and most costly ever built in Norway.'.[2]

---

[1] Ledchammer. The point of land near the house of Lede, just below Drontheim.

[2] Laing's *Heimskringla*, vol. I, p. 457. It is related that while they were planking the ship, "it happened that Thorberg had to go home to his farm upon some urgent business; and as he stayed there a long time, the ship was planked upon both sides when he came back. In the evening the king went out and Thorberg with him, to see how the ship looked, and all said that never was seen so large and fine a ship of war. Then the king went back to the town. Early the next morning the king came back again to the ship, and Thorberg with him. The carpenters were there before them, but all were standing idle with their hands across. The king asked, "What is the matter?" They said the ship was ruined; for somebody had gone from stem to stern, and cut one deep notch after another down the one side of the planking. When the king came nearer he saw that it was so, and said with an oath, 'The man shall die who has thus ruined the ship out of malice, if he can be found, and I will give a great reward to him who finds him out.' 'I can tell you, king,' says Thorberg,

Laing computes the tonnage of this ship at about nine hundred and forty-two tons, thus giving a length of about one hundred feet, which is nearly the size of a forty-two gun ship. By steam tonnage it would give a capacity of a little less than three hundred tons, and one hundred and twenty horse power. We apprehend, however, that the estimate is sufficiently large; yet we are not concerned to show any great capacity for the Icelandic ships. All the vessels employed in the early times on the American coasts were small. Cabot sailed in Baffins Bay with a vessel of thirty tons; and the Anna Pink, the craft that accompanied Lord Anson in his expedition around the world, was only sixteen tons.[1] The vessels possessed by the Northmen were everyway adapted for an ocean voyage.

In nautical knowledge, also, they were not behind the age. The importance of cultivating the study of navigation was fully understood. The Raudulf of Oesterdal, in

---

'who has done this piece of work.' 'I don't think that any one is so likely to find it out as thou art.' Thorberg says: 'I will tell you, king, who did it, I did it myself.' The king says, 'Thou must restore it all to the same condition as before, or thy life shall pay for it.' Then Thorberg went and chipped the planks until the deep notches were all smoothed and made even with the rest; and the king and all present declared that the ship was much handsomer on the side of the hull which Thorberg had chipped, and bade him shape the other side in the same way and gave him great thanks for the improvement."

[1] A few years ago two very ancient vessels which probably belonged to the seventh century were exhumed on the coast of Denmark, seven thousand feet from the sea, where they were scuttled and sunk. The changes in the coast finally left them imbedded in the sand. One vessel was seventy-two feet long, and nine feet wide amid ships. The other was forty-two feet long, and contained two eight-sided spars, twenty-four feet long. The bottoms were covered with mats of withes for the purpose of keeping them dry. Among the contents was a Damascened sword, with runes, showing that the letter existed among the Northmen in the seventh century.

Norway, taught his son to calculate the course of the sun and moon, and how to measure time by the stars. In 1520 Olaus Magnus complained that the knowledge of the people in this respect had been diminished. In that noble work called *Speculum Regale* the Icelander is taught to make an especial study of commerce and navigation, of the divisions of time and the movements of the heavenly bodies, together with arithmetic, the rigging of vessels and *morals*.[1] Without a high degree of knowledge they could never have achieved their eastern voyages.

THE DISCOVERY OF AMERICA.

We find that the Northmen were well acquainted with other parts of the world, and that they possessed all the means of reaching the continent in the west. We come, therefore, to the question: Did the Northmen actually discover and explore the coast of the country now known as America?

No one can say that the idea wears any appearance of *improbability;* for there is certainly nothing wonderful in the exploit. And after conceding the fact that the colonies of the Northmen existed in Greenland for at least three hundred years we must prepare ourselves for something of this kind. Indeed it is well nigh, if not

---

[1] The people of Iceland were always noted for their superiority in this respect over their kinsmen in Denmark and Norway. There is one significant fact bearing on this point, which is this: that, while a few of the people of Iceland went at an early period to engage in piratical excursions with the vikings of Norway, not a single pirate ship ever sailed from Iceland. Such ways were condemned altogether at an early day, while various European nations continued to sanction piracy down to recent periods. Again it should be remembered that in Iceland duelling was also solemnly declared illegal as early as 1011, and in Norway the following year; while in England it did not cease to be a part of the judicial process until 1818. See Sir Edmund Head's *Viga-Glum Saga*, p. 120.

altogether unreasonable, to suppose that a sea-faring people like the Northmen could live for three centuries within a short voyage of this vast continent, and never become aware of its existence. A supposition like this implies a rare credulity, and whoever is capable of believing it must be capable of believing almost anything.

But on this point we are not left to conjecture. The whole decision, in the absence of monuments like those of Greenland, turns upon a question of *fact*. The point is this: *Do the manuscripts which describe these voyages belong to the pre-Columbian age?* If so, then the Northmen are entitled to the credit of the prior discovery of America. That these manuscripts belong to the pre-Columbian age, is as capable of demonstration as the fact that the writings of Homer existed prior to the age of Christ. Before intelligent persons deny either of these points they must first succeed in blotting out numberless pages of well known history. The manuscript in which we have versions of all the Sagas relating to America is found in the celebrated *Codex Flatöiensis*, a work that was finished in the year 1387, or 1395 at the latest. This collection, made with great care and executed in the highest style of art, is now preserved in its integrity[1] in the archives of Copenhagen. These manuscripts were for a time supposed to be lost, but were ultimately found safely lodged in their repository in the monastery library of the island of Flatö, from whence they were transferred to Copenhagen with a

---

[1] Those who imagine that these manuscripts, while of pre-Columbian origin, have been tampered with and interpolated, show that they have not the faintest conception of the state of the question. The accounts of the voyages of the Northmen to America form the *framework* of Sagas which would actually be destroyed by the elimination of the narratives. There is only one question to be decided, and that is the *date* of these compositions.

large quantity of other literary material collected from various localities. If these Sagas which refer to America were interpolations, it would have early become apparent, as abundant means exist for detecting frauds; yet those who have examined the whole question do not find any evidence that invalidates their historical statements. In the absence, therefore, of respectable testimony to the contrary, we accept it as a fact that the Sagas relating to America are the productions of the men who gave them in their present form nearly, if not quite, an entire century before the age of Columbus.

It might also be argued, if it were at all necessary, that, if these Sagas were post-Columbian compositions drawn up by Icelanders who were jealous of the fame of the Genoese navigator, we should certainly be able to point out something either in their structure, bearing, or style by which it would be indicated. Yet such is not the case. These writings reveal no anxiety to show the connection of the Northmen with the great land lying at the west. The authors do not see anything at all remarkable or meritorious in the explorations, which were conducted simply for the purpose of gain. Those marks which would certainly have been impressed by a more modern writer forging a historical composition designed to show an occupation of the country before the time of Columbus, are wholly wanting. There is no special pleading or rivalry, and no desire to show prior and superior knowledge of the country to which the navigators had from time to time sailed. We only discover a straightforward, honest endeavor to tell the story of certain men's lives. This is done in a simple, artless way, and with every indication of a desire to mete out even handed justice to all. And candid readers who come to the subject with minds free from prejudice, will be powerfully impressed with the belief that they are reading authentic histories written by honest men.[1]

THE LITERATURE OF ICELAND.

Before speaking particularly of the substance of the Sagas it will be necessary to trace briefly the origin and history of Icelandic literature in general.

We have already mentioned the fact that Iceland was mainly settled by Norwegians of superior qualities. And this superiority was always maintained, though it was somewhat slow in manifesting itself in the form of literature. Prior to the year 1000, the Runic alphabet had existed in Iceland, but it was generally used for the simplest pur-

---

[1] The fact that Mr. Bancroft has in times past expressed opinions in opposition to this view will hardly have weight with those persons familiar with the subject. When that writer composed the first chapter of his *History of the United States*, he might have been excused for setting down the Icelandic narratives as shadowy fables; but, with all the knowledge shed upon the subject at present, we have a right to look for something better. It is therefore unsatisfactory to find him perpetuating his early views in each successive edition of the work, which show the same knowledge of the subject betrayed at the beginning. He tells us that these voyages " rest on narratives *mythological* in form, and *obscure* in meaning," which certainly cannot be the case. Furthermore they are " not contemporary;" which is true, even with regard to Mr. Bancroft's *own* work. Again, " The chief document is an interpolation in the history of Sturleson." This cannot be true in the sense intended, for Mr. Bancroft conveys the idea that the principal narrative *first* appeared in Sturleson's history when published at a *late day*. It is indeed well known that one version, but *not* the principal version, was interpolated in Peringskiold's edition of Sturleson's *Heimskringla*, printed at Copenhagen. But Bancroft teaches that these relations are of a modern date, while it is well known that they were taken *verbatim* from *Codex Flatöiensis*, finished in the year 1395. He is much mistaken in supposing that the northern Antiquarians think any more highly of the narratives in question, because they once happened to be printed in connection with Sturleson's great work. He tells us that Sturleson " could hardly have neglected the discovery of a continent," if such an event had taken place. But this, it should be remembered, depends upon

poses.¹ History and literature derived no advantage, as the runes were used chiefly for monumental inscriptions, and for mottoes and charms on such things as drinking cups, sacrifical vessels and swords. Yet the people were not without a kind of intellectual stimulus. It had long been the custom to preserve family and general histories, and recite them from memory as occasion seemed to warrant. This was done with a wonderful degree of accuracy and fidelity, by men more or less trained for the purpose, and whose performances at times were altogether surprising. They also had their scalds or poets, who were accustomed both to repeat the old songs and poems and extemporize

---

whether or not the discovery was considered of any particular importance. This does *not* appear to have been the case. The fact is nowhere dwelt upon for the purpose of exalting the actors. Besides, as Laing well observes, the discovery of land at the west had nothing to do with his subject, which was the history of the kings of Norway. The discovery of America gave rise to a little traffic, and nothing more. Moreover the kings of Norway took no part, *were not the patrons of the navigators,* and *had no influence whatever in instituting a single voyage.* Mr. Bancroft's last objection is that Vinland, the place discovered, "has been sought in all directions from Greenland and the St. Lawrence to Africa." This paragraph also conveys a false view of the subject, since the location of Vinland was as well known to the Northmen as the situation of Ireland, with which island they had uninterrupted communication. It is to be earnestly hoped that in the next edition, Mr. Bancroft may be persuaded to revise his unfounded opinions.

Washington Irving has expressed the same doubt in his Life of Columbus, *written before the means of examining this question were placed within his reach,* and in the appendix of his work he mixes the idle tales of St. Brandan's Isle with the authentic histories of the Northmen. A very limited inquiry would have led him to a different estimate.

¹ The word rune comes from *ryn,* a furrow. Odin has the credit of the invention, yet they are probably of Phenician origin. They were sometimes used for poetical purposes. Halmund, in the Grettir Saga (see Sabing Baring Gould's *Iceland*), says to his daughter: "Thou shalt now listen whilst I relate my deeds, and sing thereof a song, which thou shalt afterwards cut upon a staff." This indicates the training the memory must have undergone among the Northmen.

new ones. Every good fighter was expected to prove himself a poet when the emergency required it. This profession was strongly encouraged. When Eyvind Skialdespilder sang his great song in praise of Iceland every peasant in the island, it is said, contributed three pieces of silver to buy a clasp for his mantel of fifty marks weight. These scalds were sometimes employed by the politicians, and on one occasion a satire so nettled Harold, king of Denmark, that he sent a fleet to ravage the island, and made the repetition an offense punishable with death. These poets also went to England, to the Orkneys and to Norway, where at the king's court they were held in the highest estimation, furnishing poetical effusions on every public or private occasion which demanded the exercise of their gifts. The degree to which they had cultivated their memories was surprising. Old Blind Skald Stuf could repeat between two and three hundred poems without halting; while the Saga-men had the same power of memory, which we know may be improved to almost any extent by cultivation. But with the advent of Christianity came the Roman alphabet, which proved an easy method of expressing thought. Christianity, however, did not stop here. Its service was a reasonable service, and demanded of its votaries a high intelligence. The priest of Odin need do no more than to recite a short vow, or mutter a brief prayer. He had no divine records to read and to explain. But the minister of the new religion came with a system that demanded broader learning and culture than that implied in extemporaneous songs. His calling required the aid of books, and the very sight of such things proved a mental stimulus to this hard-brained race. Besides, Christianity opened to the minds of the people new fields of thought. These rude sons of war soon began to understand there were certain victories, not to be despised, that might be gained through peace, and soon letters came to be some what familiar to the public mind. The earliest written efforts very naturally related to the lives of the Saints, which on Sundays and holy days were read in public for the edification of the people. During the eleventh century these exercises shared the public attention with those of the professional Saga-man, who still labored to hand down the oral versions of the national history and traditions. But in the beginning of the twelfth century the use of letters was extended, and, erelong, the Saga-man found his occupation gone, the national history now being diligently gathered up by zealous students and scribes and committed to the more lasting custody of the written page. Among these was Ari Frode, who began the compilation of the Icelandic *Dooms-day Book*, which contained the records of all the early settlers. Scarcely less useful was Sæmund the Wise, who collected the poetical literature of the North and arranged it in a goodly tome. The example of these great men was followed, and by the end of the twelfth century all the Sagas relating to the pagan period of the country had been reduced to writing. This was an era of great literary activity, and the century following showed the same zeal. Finally Iceland possessed a body of prose literature superior in quantity and value to that of any other modern nation of its time.[1] Indeed, the natives of Europe at this period had no prose or other species of literature hardly worthy of the name; and, taken altogether, the Sagas formed the first prose literature in any modern language spoken by the people.[2] Says Sir Edmund Head, "No doubt there were translations in Anglo-Saxon from the Latin, by Alfred, of an earlier date, but there was in truth

---

[1] For a list of many Icelandic works, see the Introduction of Laing's *Heimskringla*.

[2] See Sir Edmund Head's *Viga Glum Saga*, pp. viii and ix.

no vernacular literature. I cannot name," he says, "any work in high or low German prose which can be carried back to this period. In France, prose writing cannot be said to have begun before the time of Villehardouin (1204), and Joinville (1202). Castilian prose certainly did not commence before the time of Alfonso X (1252). Don Juan Manvel, the author of the *Conde Lucanor*, was not born till 1282. The *Cronica General de España* was not composed till at least the middle of the thirteenth century. About the same time the language of Italy was acquiring that softness and strength which were destined to appear so conspicuously in the prose of Boccaccio, and the writers of the next century."[1]

Yet while other nations were without a literature the intellect of Iceland was in active exercise, and works were produced like the *Eddas* and the *Heimskringla*, works which being inspired by a lofty genius will rank with the writings of Homer and Herodotus while time itself endures.

But in the beginning of the sixteenth century the literature of Iceland ultimately reached the period of its greatest excellence and began to decline. Books in considerable numbers always continued to be written, though works of positive genius were wanting. Yet in Iceland there has never been an absence of literary industry, while during the recent period the national reputation has been sustained by Finn Magnussen and similar great names. One hundred years before the Plymouth colonists, following in the track of Thorwald Ericson, landed on the sands of Cape Cod, the people of Iceland had set up the printing press, and produced numerous works both in the native language and the Latin tongue.

---

[1] Ibid. Of course there was more or less poetry, yet poetry is something that is early developed among the rudest nations, while good prose tells that a people have become highly advanced in mental culture.

It is to this people, whom Saxo Grammaticus points out as a people distinguished for their devotion to letters, that we are indebted for the narratives of the pre-Columbian voyages to America. Though first arranged for oral recitation, these Sagas were afterwards committed to manuscript, the earliest of which do not now exist, and were finally preserved in the celebrated Flatö collection nearly a century before the rediscovery of America by Columbus.

But it is no longer necessary to spend much time on this point, since the character and value of the Icelandic writings have come to be so generally acknowledged, and especially since scholars and antiquarians like Humbolt have fully acknowledged their authenticity and authority.

It is proper to notice here the fact that not a few have imagined that the claims of the Northmen have been brought forward to detract from the fame of Columbus;[1] yet, nothing could be farther from the truth, since no one denies that it was by the discovery of America by Columbus that the continent first became of value to the Old World. The Northmen came and went away without accomplishing any thing of lasting value; yet, because the world at large derived no benefit from their discovery, it is certainly unjust to deny its reality.

---

[1] As early as 1411, there was a considerable trade between Bristol and Iceland, and Columbus visited Iceland in the spring of the year 1477, where he *might* have met Magnus Eyolfson, the bishop of Skalholt, or learned from some other scholar the facts in relation to the early Icelandic discoveries. Though Rafn supposes that by his visit, his opinions, previously formed regarding the existence of the Western continent, were confirmed, this is not altogether clear, for the reason that Columbus was not seeking a new continent, but a route to the Indies, which he believed he should find by sailing west. Accordingly when he found land he called it the *West* Indies, supposing that he had reached the extreme boundary of the *East* Indies. Irving tells us that Columbus founded his theory on (1), the nature of things; (2), the authority of learned writers; (3), the reports of navigators.

The fact that the Northmen knew of the existence of the Western Continent, prior to the age of Columbus, was prominently brought before the people of this country in the year 1837, when the Royal Society of Northern Antiquarians at Copenhagen published their work on the Antiquities of North America, under the editorial supervision of that great Icelandic scholar, Professor Rafn. But we are not to suppose that the first general account of these voyages was then given, for it has always been known that the history of certain early voyages to America by the Northmen were preserved in the libraries of Denmark and Iceland.[1] Torfæus, as early as 1706, published his work on Greenland, which threw much light on the subject. We find accounts of these discoveries in the works of Egede and Crantz. A very intelligent sketch, at least for those times, was given by J. Reinhold Forster, who frankly concedes the pre-Columbian discovery of America, in a *History of the Voyages and Discoveries made in the North*. Robertson speaks of them in his *History of America*, but says that he is unable to give an

---

[1] Adam of Bremen even heard of the exploits of the Northmen in Vinland, and made mention of that country. But as it *might* be said that his work did not appear until after the voyage of Columbus, and that the reference may be an interpolation, the author does not rest anything upon it. Still he unquestionably knew of the voyages of the Northmen, as he lived near the time they were made, and wrote his ecclesiastical history in about the year 1075, after he had made a visit to King Sweno of Denmark, and had accumulated much material. The passage in question is as follows: "Besides, it was stated [by the king] that a region had been discovered by many in that [the western] ocean, which was called Winland, because vines grow there spontaneously, making excellent wine; for that fruits, not planted, grow there of their own accord, we know not by false rumor, but by the certain testimony of the Danes."

The very ancient Faroese ballad of Finn the Handsome (see Rafn's *Antiquitates Americanæ*, p. 319), also contains references to Vinland, which indicates that the country was known as well by the Irish as by the Icelanders.

intelligent opinion. Indeed, the most of the older and more comprehensive writers give the Northmen recognition. Yet, owing to the fact that the Icelandic language, though simple in construction and easy of acquisition, was a tongue not understood by scholars, the subject has until recent years been suffered to lie in the back ground, and permitted, through a want of interest, to share, in a measure, the treatment meted out to vague and uncertain reports. But the well-directed efforts of the Northern Antiquarians of Denmark, supported by the enlightened zeal of scholars and historians in England, France and Germany, have done much to dispel popular ignorance, and to place the whole question in its true bearing before the people of all the principal civilized nations. In our own country, the work of Professor Rafn, already alluded to, has created a deep and wide-spread conviction of the reality of the Northman's claim, and has elicited confessions like that of Palfrey, who is obliged to say of the Icelandic records that, "their antiquity and genuineness appear to be well established, nor is there anything to bring their credibility into question, beyond the general doubt which always attaches to what is new or strange."[1]

THE NARRATIVES.

It now remains to give the reader some general account of the contents of the narratives which relate more or less to the discovery of the Western continent. In doing this, the order followed will be that which is indicated by the table of contents at the beginning of the volume.

The first extracts given are very brief. They are taken from the *Landanama Book*, and relate to the report in general circulation, which indicated one Gunnbiorn as the

---

[1] *History of New England*, vol. II, p. 53.

discoverer of Greenland, an event which has been fixed at the year 876. These fragments also give an account of a voyage to what was called Gunnbiorn's Rocks, where the adventurers passed the winter, and found in a hole, or excavation, a sum of money, which indicated that others had been there before them.

The next narrative relates to the rediscovery of Greenland by the outlaw, Eric the Red, in 983, who there passed three years in exile, and afterwards returned to Iceland. About the year 986, he brought out to Greenland a considerable colony of settlers, who fixed their abode at Brattahlid, in Ericsfiord.

Then follows two versions of the voyage of Biarne Heriulfson, who, in the same year, 986, when sailing for Greenland, was driven away during a storm, and saw a new land at the southward, which he did not visit.

Next is given three accounts of the voyage of Leif, son of Eric the Red, who in the year 1000 sailed from Brattahlid to find the land which Biarne saw. Two of these accounts are hardly more than notices of the voyage, but the third is of considerable length, and details the successes of Leif, who found and explored this new land, where he spent the winter, returning to Greenland the following spring.

After this follows the voyage of Thorvald Ericson, brother of Leif, who sailed to Vinland from Greenland, which was the point of departure in all these voyages. This expedition was begun in 1002, and it cost him his life, as an arrow from one of the natives pierced his side, causing death.

Thorstein, his brother, went to seek Vinland, with the intention of bringing home his body, but failed in the attempt, and was driven back, passing the winter in a part of Greenland remote from Brattahlid, where he died before the spring fully opened.

The most distinguished explorer was Thorfinn Karlsefne, the Hopeful, an Icelander whose genealogy runs back in the old Northern annals, through Danish, Swedish, and even Scotch and Irish ancestors, some of whom were of royal blood. In the year 1006 he went to Greenland, where he met Gudrid, widow of Thorstein, whom he married. Accompanied by his wife, who urged him to the undertaking, he sailed to Vinland in the spring of 1007, with three vessels and one hundred and sixty men, where he remained three years. Here his son Snorre was born. He afterwards became the founder of a great family in Iceland, which gave the island several of its first bishops. Thorfinn finally left Vinland because he found it difficult to sustain himself against the attacks of the natives. They spent the most of their time in the vicinity of Mount Hope Bay in Rhode Island. Of this expedition we have three narratives, all of which are given.

The next to undertake a voyage was a wicked woman named Freydis, a sister to Leif Ericson, who went to Vinland in 1011, where she lived for a time with her two ships' crews in the same places occupied by Leif and Thorfinn. Before she returned, she caused the crew of one ship to be cruelly murdered, assisting in the butchery with her own hands.

After this we have what are called the Minor Narratives, which are not essential, yet they are given that the reader may be in the possession of all that relates to the subject. The first of these refers to a voyage of Are Marson to a land southwest of Ireland, called Hvitrammana-land, or Great Ireland. This was prior to Leif's voyage to Vinland, or New England, taking place in the year 983. Biorn Asbrandson is supposed to have gone to the same place in 999. The voyage of Gudleif, who went thither, is assigned to the year 1027. The narrative of Asbrandson is given for the sake of the allusion at the close.

Finally we have a few scraps of history which speak of a voyage of Bishop Eric to Vinland in 1121, of the rediscovery of Helluland (Newfoundland) in 1285, and of a voyage to Markland (Nova Scotia) in 1347, whither the Northmen came to cut timber. With such brief notices the accounts come to an end.

THE TRUTHFULNESS OF THE NARRATIVES.

The reader will occasionally find in these narratives instances of a marvelous and supernatural character, but there is nothing at all mythological, as persons ignorant of their nature have supposed. Besides there are multitudes of narratives of a later date, to be found in all languages, which contain as many statements of a marvelous nature as these Sagas, which are nevertheless believed to contain a substantial and reliable ground-work of truth. All early histories abound in the supernatural, and these things are so well known that illustrations are hardly needed here. The relation of prodigies in no wise destroys the credibility of historical statement. If this were not so, we should be obliged to discard the greater portion of well known history, and even suspect plain matters of fact in the writings of such men as Dr. Johnson, because that great scholar fully believed in the reality of an apparition known in London as the Cock-Lane Ghost. The Sagas are as free from superstition and imagination as any other reliable narratives of that age, and just as much entitled to belief.

There will also, in certain cases, be found contradictions. The statements of the different narratives do not always coincide. The disagreements are, however, neither very numerous nor remarkable. The discrepancies are exactly what we should expect to find in a series of narratives, written at different times and by different hands.

The men who recorded the various expeditions to New England in the eleventh century agree, on the whole, quite as well as the writers of our own day, who, with vastly greater advantages, undertake to narrate the events of the second colonization in the seventeenth century.[1]

Therefore these marvelous statements and occasional contradictions in nowise detract from the historic value of the documents themselves, which, even in their very truthfulness to the times, give every evidence of authenticity and great worth. To this general appearance of truthfulness we may, however, add the force of those undesigned coincidences between writers widely separated and destitute of all means of knowing what had been already said. The same argument may be used with the Sagas which has been so powerfully employed by Paley and others in vindicating the historical character of the New Testament. In these narratives, as in those of Paul and John, it may be used with overwhelming effect. Yet we do not fear to dispense with all auxiliary aids. We are willing *to rest the whole question of the value of these narratives upon their age;* for if the Sagas date back to a period long prior to the voyage of Columbus, then the Northmen are entitled to the credit of having been the first Europeans to land upon these shores. But the date

---

[1] The liability of the best historians to fall into error, is illustrated by Paley, who shows the serious blunders in the accounts of the Marquis of Argyle's death, in the reign of Charles II: "Lord Clarendon relates that he was condemned to be *hanged*, which was performed the *same* day; on the contrary, Burnet, Woodrow, Heath, Echard concur in stating that he was *beheaded*, and that he was condemned upon Saturday and executed on Monday."—*Evidences of Christianity*, part III, chap. i. So Mr. Bancroft found it impossible to give with any accuracy the location of the French colony of St. Savion, established on the coast of Maine, by Saussaye, in 1613. Bancroft tells us that it was on the north bank of the Penobscot, while it is perfectly well known that it was located on the island of Mount Desert, a long way off in the Atlantic Ocean.

of these narratives has now been settled beyond reasonable question. The doubts of the ablest critical minds, both in Europe and America, have been effectually laid to rest, and the only reply now given to the Northern Antiquarian is some feeble paragraph pointed with a sneer.

We need not, therefore, appear before the public to cry, Place for the Northmen. They can win their *own* place, as of old. They are as strong to-day in ideas, as anciently in arms.

THE ABSENCE OF MONUMENTS AND REMAINS.

That the Northmen left no monuments or architectural remains in New England is true, notwithstanding Professor Rafn supposed that he found in the celebrated Dighton rock[1] and the stone mill at Newport, indubitable

---

[1] Dighton Rock known as the Writing Rock, is situated six and a half miles south of Taunton, Mass., on the east side of Taunton river, formed by Assonnet Neck. It lies in the edge of the river, and is left dry at low water. It is a boulder of fire graywack, twelve feet long and five feet high, and faces the bed of the river. Its front is now covered with chiseled inscriptions of what appear to be letters and outlines of men, animals and birds. As early as the year 1680, Dr. Danforth secured a drawing of the upper portion; Cotton Mather made a full copy in 1712; and in 1788, Professor Winthrop, of Harvard College, took a full-sized impression on prepared paper. Various other copies have been made at different times, all of which present substantially the same features. Yet in the interpretation of the inscription there has been little agreement. The old rock is a riddle, dumb as the Sphinx. A copy of the inscription was shown to a Mohawk chief, who decided that it was nothing less than the representation of a triumph by Indians over a wild beast which took place on this spot. Mr. Schoolcraft also showed a copy to Chingwank, an Algonquin well versed in picture-writing, who gave a similar interpretation. The Roman characters in the central part of the composition he was finally induced to reject, as having no connection with the rest. And whoever compares this inscription with those of undeniably Indian origin found elsewhere, cannot fail to be impressed with the similarity. Nevertheless, members of the Royal Society of Antiquarians, to whose notice it was

evidences of the Icelandic occupation. Any serious efforts to identify the Dighton inscription and the Newport Mill with the age of the Northmen can only serve to injure a good cause. If Professor Rafn could have seen these memorials himself, he would doubtless have been among the first to question the truth of the theory which he set forth.

In regard to the structure at Newport, Professor Rafn says that he is inclined to believe "that it had a sacred destination, and that it belonged to some monastery or Christian place of worship of one of the chief parishes in Vinland. In Greenland," he says, " there are to be found ruins of several round buildings in the vicinity of the churches. One of this description, in diameter about twenty-six feet, is situated at the distance of three hundred feet to the eastward of the great church in Igalliko;

---

brought by the Rhode Island Historical Society, felt strongly persuaded that the rock bears evidence of the Northman's visit to these shores. Mr. Laing, the accomplished translator of the *Heimskringla*, in discussing the theories in regard to the inscription, says, that the only real resemblance to letters is found in the middle of the stone, in which antiquarians discover the name of Thorfinn, that is, Thorfinn Karlsefne, the leader of the expedition which came to New England in 1007. Just over these letters is a character supposed to be Roman also, which may signify NA, or MA, the letter A being formed by the last branch of M. Now MA in Icelandic is used as an abbreviation of *Madr*, which signifies the original settler of a country. Close to these two letters are several numerals, construed to mean *one hundred and fifty-one*. And according to the account of the voyage, Thorfinn lost *nine* of the hundred and sixty men with whom it is presumed he started, and therefore one *hundred and fifty-one* would exactly express the number with him at the time he is supposed to have cut the inscription. This, then, would mean altogether, that Thorfinn Karlsefne established himself here with one hundred and fifty-one men. Yet, as the testimony of this rock is not needed, we may readily forego any advantage that can be derived from its study. Besides, the history of similar cases should serve to temper our zeal. In the time of Saxo Grammatticus (1160), there was a stone at Hoby, near Runamoe, in the Swedish province of Bleking, which was supposed to be sculptured with runes. At a late day another of forty-four feet in diameter, at the distance of four hundred and forty feet to the eastward of the church in Karkortok; .... a third, of thirty-two feet diameter amongst the ruins of sixteen buildings at Kanitsok."[1] He supposes that all these ancient remains of the Icelanders, which are to be seen in Greenland to-day, are baptisteries, similar to those of Italy.

According to this view, there must have been a considerable ecclesiastical establishment in Vinland, which is not clearly indicated by the Sagas, from which we learn no more than the simple fact that Bishop Eric sailed on a voyage to this place in the year 1121. But is it probable that the Northmen would have erected a baptistery like

---

copies were furnished the antiquarians, who came to the conclusion, as Laing tells us, that it was a genuine inscription, referring to the battle of Braaville, fought in the year 680. It afterwards turned out that the apparent inscription was made by the disintegration of veins of a soft material existing in the rock. Yet the Dighton inscription is beyond question the work of man. Mr. A. E. Kendal, writing in 1807, says that there was a tradition that Assonnet Neck, on which tongue of land the rock is situated, was once a place of banishment among the Indians. He states, further, that the Indians had a tradition to the effect, that in ancient times some *white* men in a *bird* landed there and were slaughtered by the aborigines. They also said thunder and lightening issued from the bird, which fact indicates that this event, if it occurred at all, must be referred to the age of gunpowder. Mr. Kendal mentions the story of a ship's anchor having been found there at an early day. In former years the rock was frequently dug under by the people, in the hope of finding concealed treasures. It is said that a small rock once existed near by which also bore marks of human hands. The Portsmouth and Tiverton Rocks, described by Mr. Webb (*Antiquitates Americanæ*, pp. 355-71), are doubtless Indian inscriptions; while that on the island of Monhegan, off the coast of Maine, may perhaps be classed with the rock of Hoby. Yet after all, it is possible that the *central* portion of the inscription on the Dighton Rock, may be the work of the Northmen. That two distinct parties were concerned in making the inscription is clear from the testimony of the Indians, who did not pretend to understand the portion thought to refer to Karlsefne. For the full discussion, see *Antiquitates Americanæ*, p. 378, *et seq*.

[1] *Memoirs des Antiquaires du Nord*, 1839-9, p. 377.

this, and, at the same time, left no other monument? It seems hardly reasonable. Besides, whoever examines this ancient structure must be impressed by its modern aspect, so especially apparent in the preservation of the mortar, which does not bear the marks of seven centuries. The displacement of a portion of the masonry might perhaps reveal some peculiarity that would effectually settle the question of its antiquity to the satisfaction of all.[1]

In treating this subject we shall run into needless errors and difficulties, if we attempt the task of discovering monuments of the Northmen in New England. In Greenland these evidences of their occupation are abundant, because they were regularly established on the ground for generations, and formed their public and private edifices of the only material at hand, which was well nigh imperishable. But their visits to New England were comparatively few, and were scattered over many years. Owing to the weakness of their numbers, they found

---

[1] The Old Mill at Newport stands on an eminence in the centre of the town, being about twenty-four feet high, and twenty-three feet in diameter. It rests upon eight piers and arches. It has four small windows, and, high up the wall, above the arches, was a small fire place. It is first distinctly mentioned in the will of Governor Benedict Arnold, of Newport, where it is called, "my stone-built wind mill." It is known that during the eighteenth century it served both as a mill and powder house. Edward Pelham, who married Governor Arnold's granddaughter, in 1740 also called it "an old stone mill." Peter Easton, who early went to live in Newport, wrote in 1663, that "this year we built the first windmill;" and August 28, 1675, he says, "A storm blew down our windmill." What Easton relates occurred before Governor Arnold writes about his stone windmill, and it is not unreasonable to suppose that when the one spoken of by Easton was destroyed he built something more substantial. Yet we cannot say that this was actually the case. The old tower existing at the beginning of the settlement may have been adapted by him for the purposes of a mill, when the one mentioned by Easton was destroyed.

The family of the Governor is said to have come from Warwickshire, England, and one of his farms was called the Leamington farm, as is supposed,

permanent colonies impracticable. Thorfinn Karlsefne deliberately gave up the attempt at the end of a three years experiment, saying that it would be impossible to maintain themselves against the more numerous bands of natives. Their habitations were temporary. The various companies that came into Vinland, instead of building new houses, took possession of Leif's booths, and simply added others like them when they afforded insufficient quarters. To ask for monuments of the Northmen is therefore unreasonable, since their wooden huts and timber crosses must soon have disappeared. The only memorial we have a right to expect is some trifling relic, a coin or amulet, perhaps, that chance may yet throw in the antiquarian's way.[1] In the meanwhile among scholars the

---

from the place by that name near Warwick. In addition to this, in the Chesterton Parish, three miles from Leamington, there is an old windmill similar in construction to that at Newport. It is supposed that it was erected on pillars for pneumatic reasons, and also that carts might thus go underneath and be loaded and unloaded with greater ease. And it has been suggested, that *if* Gov. Arnold came from Warwickshire, of which the proof is not given, and *if* the Chesterton Mill was standing at the time of his departure for New England, he might have built a mill at Newport after the same model. Yet this is something we know little about. And whence came the Chesterton Mill itself? There was a *tradition* that it was built after a design by Inigo Jones, but this is only a tradition. That structure also might have belonged to the class of Round Towers in Ireland, of which one at least was built by Northmen. All is therefore, in a measure, doubtful. It will hardly help the Northmen to class this Newport relic with their works. See Palfrey's *New England*, vol. I, pp. 57-9.

[1] Many have supposed that the skeleton in armor, dug up near Fall River, was a relic of the Northmen, and one of those men killed by the natives in the battle with Karlsefne. But it would be far more reasonable to look for traces of the Northmen among the Indians of Gaspé, who, at an early day, were distinguished for an unusual degree of civilization. Malte Brun tells us that they worshiped the sun, knew the points of the compass, observed the position of some of the stars, and traced maps of their country. Before the French missionaries went among

Icelandic narratives are steadily winning their way to unquestioned belief. This is all the more gratifying in an age like the present, in which large portions of history are being dismissed to the realms of hoary fable, and all the annals of the past are being studied in a critical spirit, with true aims and a pure zeal.

---

them they worshiped the figure of the Cross, and had a tradition that a venerable person once visited them, and during an epidemic cured many by the use of that symbol. See Malte Brun's *Geography* (English edition), vol. v, p. 135. Malte Brun's authority is Father Leclerc's *Nouvelle Relation de la Gaspesie*, Paris, 1672.

THE MAJOR NARRATIVES.

PRE-COLUMBIAN DISCOVERY.

I. FRAGMENTS FROM LANDNAMA-BOK.

The following extracts from the *Landnama*,[1] give us the earliest information on record, in regard to the westward movements of the Icelanders. The men referred to were well known, and the mention of their names and exploits in this great work, than which no higher authority could be produced, is gratifying. These extracts, which are given in the order in which they stand in vol. I. of *Grönland's Historiske Mindesmærker*, the greater portion of which work is the labor of Finn Magnusen, have probably never appeared before in an English dress. The first extract simply mentions Gunnbiorn and his Rocks; the second shows that Eric the Red obtained his knowledge of the existence of Greenland through this person; the third again gives the name of Gunnbiorn: while the fourth furnishes a brief account of an early voyage to the Rocks. It appears from these references, that, previous to the sail-

---

[1] *The Landnama-bok*. This is probably the most complete record of the kind ever made by any nation. It is of the same general character as the English *Doomsday Book*, but vastly superior in interest and value. It contains the names of three thousand persons and one thousand four hundred places. It gives a correct account of genealogies of the first settlers, with brief notices of their achievements. It was commenced by the celebrated Frode, the Wise, who was born 1067, and died 1148, and was continued by Kalstegg, Styrmer and Thordsen, and completed by Hauk Erlendson, *Lagman*, or Governor of Iceland, who died in the year 1334.

ing of Eric the Red, the existence of land at the west was well understood, the report of Gunnbiorn's adventure having been quite generally circulated amongst the people.

---

1. There was a man named Grimkel, [A. D. 876.] son of Ulf Hreidarson, called Krage, and brother to Gunnbiorn,[1] after whom Gunnbiorn's Rocks[2] are named. He took possession of that piece of land that extends from Berevigs Röin to Ness Röin, and out round the point of the cape. And he lived on Saxahval. He drove away Saxe, a son of Alfarin Valeson, and he lived on the Röin of Saxahval. Alfarin Valeson had first taken possession of the cape between Berevigs Röin and Enne.

2. Eric Red [A. D. 983.] said that he intended to find the land that was seen by Gunnbiorn,[3] Ulf Krage's son, when he was driven by a storm west from Iceland, and

---

[1] Gunnbiorn appears to have been a Northman who settled in Iceland at an early day. Nothing more is known of him.

[2] Torfæus says that these rocks lie six sea miles out from Geirfuglesker, out from Reikiavek, and twelve miles south of Garde in Greenland, yet they cannot now be found. It is not too much to suppose that they have been sunk by some of those fearful convulsions which have taken place in Iceland; yet it is quite as reasonable to conclude that these rocks were located elsewhere, probably nearer the east coast, which was formerly more accessible than now. In the version of the Account of Greenland, by Ivar Bardason (see *Antiquitates Americanæ*, p. 301), given from a *Faroese Manuscript*, and curiously preserved by Purchas, *His Pilgrimage*, vol. III, p. 518, we read as follows:

"*Item.* men shall know, that, between *Island* and *Greenland*, lyeth a Risse called *Gornbornse-Skare*. There were they wont to haue their passage for *Gronland*. But as they report there is Ice upon the same Risse, come out of the Long North Bottome, so that we cannot use the same old Passage as they thinke."

[3] Torfæus says (*Greenlandia*, p. 73), that "Eric the Red first lived in Greenland, but it was discovered by the man called Gunnbiorn. After him Gunnbiorn's Rocks are called."

found Gunnbiorn's Rocks. [A.D. 876.] At the same time he said if he did not find the land he would return to his friends.

3. Two sons of Gunnbiorn, Ulf Krage's son, after whom Gunnbiorn's Rocks were named, were called Gunstein and Haldor. They took possession of Skötufiorden, Löigardelen and Ogursvigen to Mjorfiord. Berse was Haldor's son, father to Thormod Kalbrunarskald.

Snæbiorn (Holmstein's son), called Galte, owned a ship [A. D. 970.] that lay in the mouth of Grimsar (in Borgafiorden). Rolf, from Rödesand, bought a half of the ship. Each of the parties mustered twelve men. With Snæbiorn, was Thorkel and Sumarlide, sons of Thorgier Red, son of Einar, from Stafholdt.

Snæbiorn also took Thorod from Thingness, his stepfather and his five sons, and Rolf took Stærbiorn. The last named recited the following verse, after he had a dream:

> Both ours
> dead I see;
> all empty
> in Northwestern Sea;
> cold weather,
> great suffering,
> I expect
> Snæbiorn's death.[1]

They sought Gunnbiorn's Rocks and found land. Snæbiorn would not permit any one to go ashore in the night. Stærbiorn landed, notwithstanding, and found a purse[2]

---

[1] The translation is literal or nearly so, and the sense is obscure.

[2] This shows that others had been there before. They were doubtless Icelanders who were sailing to Greenland. The place of concealment appears to have been an excavation covered with stone or wood. That the people were sometimes accustomed to hide money in this way, is evident.

with money in an earth hole, and concealed it. Snæbiorn hit him with an axe so that the purse fell down.

They built a cabin to live in, and it was all covered with snow. Thorkel Red's son, found that there was water on a shelf that stood out of the cabin window. This was in the month of Goe.[1] They shovelled the snow away. Snæbiorn rigged the ship; Thorod and five of his party were in the hut, and Stærbiorn and several men of Rolf's party. Some hunted.[2] Stærbiorn killed Thorod, but both he and Rolf killed Snæbiorn. Red's sons and all the rest

---

We read in the Saga of Eric the Red, that this person at first intended to go with his son, Leif, on his voyage to discover the land seen by Heriulf, and which Leif named Vinland. On his way to the ship, Eric's horse stumbled, and he fell to the ground seriously injured, and was obliged to abandon the voyage. He accepted this as a judgment for having, as one preparation for his absence, buried his money, where his wife, Thorhild, would not be able to find it.

[1] This is believed to have been about February, which affords one of many indications that the climate of that region has become more rigorous than formerly. The fact that water did not freeze, indicates mild weather, which we might infer from the rigging of their vessels, and the preparation for sea. In regard to the term Goe, *Grönland's Historiske Mindesmærker* (vol. *s*, p. 7), says: "This name was before used in Denmark, which Etatsraad Werlauf has discovered on the inscription of a Danish Rune-Stone."

[2] The facts that they engaged in hunting, and that they built a cabin to live in, might at first lead some to suppose that the place contained a forest or more or less trees, to supply wood. Yet this does not follow, as drift wood might supply all their wants for building purposes, where they could not obtain or use stone. Regarding drift wood, Crantz says, in speaking of Greenland: "For as He has denied this frigid, rocky region the growth of trees, He has bid the storms of the ocean to convey to its shores a great deal of wood, which accordingly comes floating thither, part without ice, but the most part along with it, and lodges itself between the islands. Were it not for this, we Europeans should have no wood to burn there. . . . Among this wood are great trees torn up by the roots, which by driving up and down for many years, and dashing and rubbing on the ice, are quite bare of branches. A small part of this drift wood are willows, alder and birch trees, which come out of the bays in the south; also large trunks of aspen trees, . . . but the greatest part is pine and fir. We find also, a good deal of a sort of wood, finely veined, and with few branches; this, I fancy, is

were obliged to take the oath of allegiance to save their lives. They arrived on their return at Helgeland, Norway, and later at Vadil in Iceland.[1]

II. THE COLONIZATION OF GREENLAND.

The first document relating to the settlement of Greenland by the Northmen, is taken from the Saga of Eric the Red, as given in Professor Rafn's *Antiquitates Americanæ*. Besides the history of Eric and his sons, that Saga contains notices of other voyages. The following are simply extracts. The whole Saga does not necessarily apply to the subject under examination — the Discovery of America. The second extract, which gives more of the particulars, is from *Grönland's Historiske Mindesmærker*, vol. II, p. 201. The third is also taken from the same great historical depository.

FIRST NARRATIVE.

There was a man named Thorvald, son of Osvald, son of Ulf-Ocxna-Thorerisson. Thorvald and his son were obliged to leave Jardar[2] and go to Iceland, on account of manslaughter. At that time Iceland was generally colo-

---

larchwood. . . . . There is also a solid, reddish wood of a more agreeable fragrancy than the common fir, with visible cross veins, which I take to be the same species as the beautiful silver firs, or zirbel, that have the smell of cedar, and grow on the high Grison hills, and the Switzers wainscot ther rooms with them."—*History of Greenland*, vol. I, p. 37.

[1] If any confirmation were needed of the truth of this narrative, or of the killing of Snæbiorn and Thorod, we might look for it in the equally well known fact, that after the return of the voyagers to Iceland, the death of these two men was fearfully revenged by their friends.

[2] In the southwest of Norway.

nized.[1] They first lived in Drangey, where Thorvald died. Then Eric married Thorhild, daughter of Jorund and Thorbiarg Knarrabringa, whom afterwards Thorbiorn of Haukdale married. Eric moved from the north, and fixed his abode in Ericstad opposite Vatshorn. The son of Eric and Thorhold was named Leif. But after Eyulf Soers and Holm-Gang Rafn's murder, Eric was banished from Haukdale. Eric went westward to Breidafiord and lived at Oexney in Ericstad. He lent Thorgest his seat-posts,[2] and he could not get them again. He then demanded them. Then came disputes and hostility between him and Thorgest, which is told in the history of Eric. Styr Thorgrim's son, Eyulf of Svinoe, the sons of Brand of Aptelfiord and Thorbiorn Vifilsson plead the cause of Eric; Thorder Gellurson and Thorgeir of Hitardale plead for Thorgest. Eric was declared outlawed by the Thing, and prepared his ship for sea in Eric's Bay. Styr and the others went with him beyond the island. [A.D. 982.] Then Eric declared it to be his resolution to seek the land which Gunnbiorn, Ulf Krage's son, saw [A. D. 876.] when driven into the Western ocean, where he found Gunnbiorn's Rocks, saying, that if he did not find the land he would return to his friends. Eric set sail from Snæfellsjokul, and found land which from its height he called Midjokul, now called Blaaserk. Thence he sailed along the shore in a southerly direction, seeking for the nearest habitable land. The first winter he passed in Ericseya,[3] near the middle of the east district. The following year he came into Ericsfiord, where he

---

[1] See Colonization of Iceland, in the Introduction.

[2] See notes to Introduction.

[3] It is now impossible to identify these localities. The old view, that what is called the East-bygd, or District, was on the eastern coast of Greenland, is now abandoned. It is probable that no settlement was ever effected on the east coast, though once it was evidently more approachable than now. See Graah's *Expedition*.

fixed his seat. The same summer he explored the western desert, and gave names to many places. The following winter he passed on a holm opposite Rafnsgnipa, and the third year he came into Iceland and brought his ship into Breidafiord. The land which he found, he named Greenland, saying that men would be persuaded to go to a land with so good a name. Eric stayed in Iceland that winter, and the summer after he went over to the land which he had found, and fixed his abode in Brattahlid in Ericsfiord. [A. D. 986.] Men acquainted with affairs, say, that this same summer in which Eric went to settle in Greenland, thirty-five ships sailed from Breidafiord and Bogafjord, of which only fourteen arrived, and the rest were driven back or lost. This event took place fifteen winters[1] before the Christian religion was established in Iceland. The same summer, Bishop Frederick and Thorvold Kodranson went from Iceland.[2] Among those who emigrated with Eric and established themselves, were Heriulf Heriulfsfiord who took Heriulfsness, and abode in Heriulfsness, Ketil Ketilsfiord, Rafn Rafnsfiord, Solvi Solvidale, Helgi Thorbrandson Alptafiord, Thorbjornglora Siglefjord, Einar Einarsfiord, Hafgrim Hafgrimsfiord and Vatnahver, Arnlaug Arnlaugsfiord; and other men went to the west district.

The Baptism of Leif the Fortunate.

And when the sixth[3] winter had passed [A. D. 999.] since Eric Red went to live in Greenland, Leif, son of Eric, went over from Greenland to Norway, and in the autumn

---

[1] As we certainly know that Christianity was established in Iceland in the year A. D. 1000, the final settlement of Eric and his followers must have taken place during the year assigned, viz: 985.

[2] See *Antiquitates Americanæ*, p. 15, note a.

[3] Evidently an error. See *Antiquitates Americanæ*, p. 15, note 3.

arrived in Throndheim and came north to King Olaf Trygvesson,[1] from Hegeland. He brought his ship to Nidaros and went at once to King Olaf. The king commanded Leif and some other pagan men to come to him. They were exhorted to accept religion, which the king having easily arranged with Leif, he and all his sailors were baptized, and passed the winter with the king, being liberally entertained.

SECOND NARRATIVE.

Thorvold the son of Usvold, son of Ulf, son of Oexne-Thorer, and his son, Eric Red, left Jardar in Norway on account of manslaughter, and took possession of a piece of land on Hornastrand [Iceland], and lived there at Drangey. There Thorvold died. Eric then married Thorhild, daughter of Jorund Atleson and Thorbiarg Knarrabringa, who was then married to Thorbiorn of Haukdale. Then Eric went from the north and ploughed the fields in Haukdale. Then he lived in Ericstadt by Vatshorn. There his thralls[2] let a piece of rock tumble down over Valthiof's

---

[1] This king propagated Christianity by physical force, and marked the course of his missionary tours with fire and blood; which might have been expected from a barbarian just converted from the worship of Odin and Thor.

[2] These thralls were slaves, though slavery in Iceland assumed peculiar features. The following from the *Saga of Gisli the Outlaw*, shows the relation that slaves held to freemen. We read, that on one occasion, Gisli had borrowed a famous sword of Koll, and the latter asked to have it back, but Gisli in reply asks if he will sell it, receiving a negative reply. Then he says: "I will give thee thy freedom and goods, so that thou mayest fare whither thou wilt with other men." This is also declined, when Gisli continues: "Then I will give thee thy freedom, and lease, or give thee land, and besides I will give thee sheep, and cattle and goods, as much as thou needest." This he also declines, and Kol, when Gisli asks him to name a price, offering any sum of money, besides his freedom, and "a becoming match, if thou hast a liking for any one." But Kol refused to

house in Valthiofstadt. But his relation, Eyulf Söirs, killed the thralls at Kneide-Brinke above Vatshorn. For this cause, Eric killed Eyulf Söirs. He also killed Holm-Gang Rafn at Leikskaale. Geirstein and Odd at Jörund Eyulf Söirs relations brought a suit against the slayer. Eric was then banished from Hauksdale, and took possession of the islands, Brokö and Oexno, but lived in Todum at Sydero, the first winter. Then he loaned Thorgest his seat-posts. Then Eric moved to Oexno and lived in Ericstadt. Then he demanded his seat-posts, but did not get them. Eric took them thereafter from Bredobolstad, but Thorgest followed him. They fought near the house at Drangey. Two sons of Thorgest fell, and some other men. Thereafter they both kept their followers with them. Styr, Eyulf of Svino, Thorbrand's sons of Alptefiord, and Thorbiorn Vifilsson, were of Eric's party. But Thord Gelleirson, Thorgeir from Hitardale, Aslak of Langedale, and Illuge's son helped Thorgest. Eric and his party were sentenced to be banished at Thorsness Thing. He fitted out a ship in Ericsfiord, but Eyulf concealed him in Dimonsvaag, while Thorgest and his men sought after him on the highlands. Thorbiorn, Eyulf and Styr followed with Eric out to sea beyond the islands. He said that he meant to seek the land Gunnbiorn, Ulf Krage's son, saw [A. D. 876.] when he was driven by a storm west from Iceland, and found Gunnbiorn's Rocks; though he said at the same time if he discovered the land he would return to his friends. [A. D. 982.] Eric laid his course to the west from Snæfieldness, and approached [Greenland] from the sea to

---

sell it at any price, which refusal led to a fight, and in the first onset, the slave's axe sank into Gisli's brain, while the disputed sword, *Graysteel*, clove the thick skull of Kol. See the *Saga of Gisli the Outlaw*, p, 6, Edinburgh, 1866. Also the Saga of Eric Red, where Thorbiorn thinks it an indignity that Einar should ask for the hand of his daughter in marriage, Einar being the son of a slave.

land at Midjokul, in that place that is called Blæsark. From thence he went along the coast to the south, to see if the land was fit to live in. The first year he stayed all winter in Ericksö, nearly in the middle of the west bygd. In the next spring [A. D. 983.] he went to Ericsfiord, and there found a dwelling. Next summer he went to the western bygd, and gave certain names to many places. The second winter he lived in Ericsholm, at Hvarfo Fiedspidæ, and at the third summer [A. D. 984.] he went north to Snæfield, inside of Rafnsfiord. He thought then that the place where Ericsfiord bent was opposite the place where he came. He then returned and spent the third winter in Ericksö opposite the mouth of Ericsfiord. The next summer [A. D. 985.] he went to Iceland, and landed at Breidafiord. The next winter he stayed at Holmstater, with Ingolf. Next spring he fought with Thorgest and lost the battle. That summer, Eric began to settle the land which he had discovered [A. D. 986.] and which he called Greenland, because he said that the people would not like to move there, if the land did not have a good name. Learned men say that twenty-five ships went that summer to Greenland from Breidafiord and Borgafjord, but only fourteen arrived. Of the rest, some were driven back and others were wrecked. This happened fifteen winters before Christianity was introduced into Iceland.

THIRD NARRATIVE.

The land some call Greenland, was discovered and settled from Iceland. Eric the Red was the name of the Breidafiord man, who [A. D. 986.] went from here [Iceland] to there, and took possession of that part of the land, which later was called Ericsfiord. He named the land and called it Greenland, and said it would encourage people to come there, if the land had a good name. They found there, both east and west, ruins of houses and pieces of boats, and begun stonework. From which it is to be seen what kind of people have lived in Vinland, and which the Greenlanders call Skrælings and who had been there. He [Eric] began to settle the land fourteen or fifteen years before the introduction of Christianity in Iceland. Afterwards this was told of Greenland to Thorkel Gelleirson, by a man who had himself followed Eric Red.

III. THE VOYAGE OF BIARNE.

The voyage of Biarne to Greenland was attended by many hardships. His vessel was blown away from the course during a storm, at which time he saw the shores of the American continent, yet he made no attempt to land. Of this voyage we have two versions. The first is a translation of a passage from *Codex Flatöiensis*, given in *Antiquitates Americanæ*, p. 17. The second is taken from *Grönland's Historiske Mindesmærker*. The date of this voyage is fixed by the fact that Biarne sailed the same season that his father settled in Greenland, which, as we learn from the narrative of Eric, was in the year 985. There is a complete agreement between this account and the preceding.

FIRST NARRATIVE.

Heriulf was the son of Bard, Heriulf's son, who was a relation of Ingolf the Landnamsman.[1] Ingolf gave Heriulf land between Vog and Reikianess. Heriulf dwelt first at Dropstock. His wife was called Thorgird, and their son

---

[1] Original settler or freeholder, whose name and possessions were recorded in the *Landnama-bok*.

was called Biarne. He was a promising young man. In his earliest youth he had a desire to go abroad, and he soon gathered property and reputation; and was by turns a year abroad, and a year with his father. Biarne was soon in possession of a merchant ship of his own. The last winter [A. D. 985.] while he was in Norway, Heriulf prepared to go to Greenland with Eric, and gave up his dwelling. There was a Christian man belonging to the Hebudes along with Heriulf, who composed the lay called the *Hafgerdingar*[1] Song, in which is this stave:

> May he whose hand protects so well
> The simple monk in lonely cell,
> And o'er the world upholds the sky,
> His own blue hall, still stand me by.[2]

Heriulf settled at Heriulfness [A. D. 985.] and became a very distinguished man. Eric Red took up his abode at Bratthalid, and was in great consideration, and honored by all. These were Eric's children: Leif, Thorvold, and Thorstein; and his daughter was called Ferydis. She was married to a man called Thorvald; and they dwelt at Gardar, which

---

[1] This poem no longer exists. Its subject, the *Hafgerdingar*, is described as a fearful body of water, "which sometimes rises in the sea near Greenland in such a way that three large rows of waves inclose a part of the sea, so that the ship that finds itself inside, is in the greatest danger."—*Grönland's Historiske Mindismærker*, vol. I, p. 264. There does not appear to be any better foundation for this notion of the Hafgerdingar than of the old accounts of the Maelstrom, once supposed to exist on the coast of Norway. The Hafgardingar may have originated from seeing the powerful effect of a cross sea acting on the tide.

[2] To this translation may be added another in metre, by Beamish:

> O thou who triest holy men!
> Now guide me on my way;
> Lord of the earth's wide vault, extend
> Thy gracious hand to me.

This appears to be the earliest Christian prayer thus far found in connection with this period of American history.

is now a bishop's seat. She was a haughty, proud woman; and he was but a mean man. She was much given to gathering wealth. The people of Greenland were heathen at this time. Biarne came over the same summer [A. D. 985.] with his ship to the strand[1] which his father had sailed abroad from in the spring. He was much struck with the news, and would not unload his vessel. When his crew asked him what he intended to do, he replied that he was resolved to follow his old custom by taking up his winter abode with his father. "So I will steer for Greenland if ye will go with me." They one and all agreed to go with him. Biarne said, "Our voyage will be thought foolish, as none of us have been on the Greenland sea before." Nevertheless they set out to sea as soon as they were ready, and sailed for three days, until they lost sight of the land they left. But when the wind failed, a north wind with fog set in, and they knew not where they were sailing to; and this lasted many days. At last they saw the sun, and could distinguish the quarters of the sky; so they hoisted sail again, and sailed a whole day and night, when they made land. They spoke among themselves what this land could be, and Biarne said that, in his opinion, it could not be Greenland. On the question, if he should sail nearer to it, he said, "It is my advice that we sail up close to the land." They did so; and they soon saw that the land was without mountains, was covered with woods, and that there were small hills inland. They left the land on the larboard side, and had their sheet on the land side.

---

[1] *Æyrar.* This is not the name of a place — for Heriulf dwelt in Iceland at a place called Dropstock — but of a natural feature of ground; *eyri,* still called an ayre in the Orkney islands, being a flat, sandy tongue of land, suitable for landing and drawing up boats upon. All ancient dwellings in those islands, and probably in Iceland also, are situated so as to have the advantage of this kind of natural wharf, and the spit of land called an ayre, very often has a small lake or pond inside of it, which shelters boats.—*Laing.*

Then they sailed two days and nights before they got sight of land again. They asked Biarne if they thought this would be Greenland; but he gave his opinion that the land was no more Greenland, than the land they had seen before. "For on Greenland, it is said, there are great snow mountains." They soon came near to the land, and saw that it was flat and covered with trees. Now, as the wind fell, the ship's people talked of its being advisable to make for the land; but Biarne would not agree to it. They thought that they would need wood and water; but Biarne said: "Ye are not in want of either." And the men blamed him for this. He ordered them to hoist the sail, which was done. They now turned the ship's bow from the land, and kept the sea for three days and nights, with a fine breeze from southwest. Then they saw a third land, which was high and mountainous, and with snowy mountains. Then they asked Biarne if he would land here; but he refused altogether: "For in my opinion this land is not what we want."[1] Now they let the sails stand and kept along the land and saw it was an island. Then they turned from the land and stood out to sea with the same breeze; but the gale increased, and Biarne ordered a reef to be taken in, and not to sail harder than the ship and her tackle could easily bear. After sailing three days and nights, they made, the fourth time, land;

---

[1] The details of this voyage are very simple, yet whoever throws aside his old time prejudices, and considers the whole subject with the care which it deserves, cannot otherwise than feel persuaded that Biarne was driven upon this Continent, and that the land seen was the coast of that great territory which stretches between Massachusetts and Newfoundland, for there is no other land to answer the description. Of course, no particular merit can be claimed for this discovery. It was also accidental, something like the discovery of America by Columbus, who, in looking for the East Indies, stumbled upon a new world. Yet Biarne's discovery soon led to substantial results.

and when they asked Biarne if he thought this was Greenland or not, Biarne replies: "This is most like what has been told me of Greenland; and here we shall take to the land." They did so, and came to the land in the evening, under a ness, where they found a boat. On this ness dwelt Biarne's father, Heriulf; and from that it is called Heriulfness. Biarne went to his father's, gave up seafaring, and after his father's death, continued to dwell there when at home.

SECOND NARRATIVE.

A man named Heriulf, son of Bard, son of Heriulf, a relation to Landnamsman Ingolf, who gave the last named Heriulf the piece of land that lies between Vaag and Reikianess. The younger Heriulf went to Greenland, when Eric Red began to settle there, and on his ship was a Christian man from the South Islands [the Hebrides] who was the author of the poem, *Havgerdingar*, in which was the following verse :

> I to the monk's protector pray
> That he will give my voyage luck!
> The heaven's great Ruler
> Save me from danger.

Heriulf took possession of Heriulfsfiord, and became one of the chief men. Eric Red took to himself Ericsfiord, and lived in Brattahlid, and Leif, his son, after his death. Those men who at the same time went away with Eric took possession of the following pieces of land: Heriulf Heriulfsfiord, and he lived in Heriulfness, Ketil Ketilsfiord, Rafn Rafnsfiord, Sölve Sölvedale, Snorro Thorbrandson Alptefiord, Thorbiornglora Siglefiord, Einar Einarsfiord, Havgrim Havgrimsfiord and Vatnahverf, Arnlaug Arnlaugfiord; but some went to the west bygd. A man named

Thorkel Forsark, cousin to Eric Red on their mother's side, went to Greenland with Eric, and took possession of Hvalsöfiord, together with the greater part of the piece of land between Eyolfsfiord and Einarsfiord, and lived in Hvalosöfne. From him came the Hvalsöfiord people. He was very strong. Once Eric Red visited him, and he would welcome his guest in the best way possible, but he had no boats at hand which he could use. He was compelled to swim out to Hvalsö, and get a full-grown sheep,[1] and carry it on his back home to his house. It was a good half mile. Thorkel was buried in a cave in the field of Hvalsöfiord.

IV. LEIF'S VOYAGE TO VINLAND.

This voyage is recorded in the *Flatö Manuscript*, and is given in *Antiquitates Americanæ*, pp. 26–40. It contains the account of the voyage of Leif, son of Eric the Red, who, following out the hints of Biarne, sailed to discover the

---

[1] Considerable has been said at various times in opposition to these accounts, because cattle and sheep, and sometimes horses, are mentioned in connection with Greenland. Some have supposed that, for these reasons, the Saga must be incorrect. Yet, in more modern times, there has been nothing to prevent the people from keeping such animals, though it has been found better to substitute dogs for horses. Crantz says, that in "the year 1759, one of our missionaries brought three sheep with him from Denmark to New Herrnhuth. These have so increased by bringing some two, some three lambs a year, that they have been able to kill some every year since, to send some to Lichtenfels, for a beginning there, and, after all, to winter ten at present. We may judge how vastly sweet and nutritive the grass is here, from the following tokens: that tho' three lambs come from one ewe, they are larger, even in autumn, than a sheep of a year old in Germany." He says that in the summer they could pasture two hundred sheep around New Herrnhuth; and that they formerly kept cows, but that it proved too much trouble.—*History of Greenland*, vol. I, p. 74.

new land, which he called Vinland, on account of the quantity of vines that he found growing wild. Several extracts are appended, because of interest in connection with the subject.

[A. D. 984.] It is next to be told that Biarne Heriulfson came over from Greenland to Norway, on a visit to Earl Eric, who received him well. Biarne tells of this expedition of his, in which he had discovered unknown land; and people thought he had not been very curious to get knowledge, as he could not give any account of those countries, and he was somewhat blamed on this account. [A. D. 986.] Biarne was made a Court man of the earl, and the summer after he went over to Greenland; and afterwards there was much talk about discovering unknown lands. Leif, a son of Eric Red of Brattahlid, went over[1] to Biarne Heriulfson, and bought the ship from him, and manned the vessel, so that in all, there were thirty-five men on board. Leif begged his father Eric to go as commander of the expedition; but he excused himself, saying he was getting old, and not so able as formerly to undergo the hardship of a sea voyage. Leif insisted that he among all their relations was the most likely to have good luck on such an expedition; and Eric consented, and rode from home with Leif, when they had got all ready for sea; but when they were coming near to the ship,[2] the horse on which Eric

---

[1] He must have gone over to Greenland from Norway then, as in the year 1000, he returned and introduced Christianity into Greenland. The language used is indefinite.

[2] One recension of the Saga of Eric the Red, states that he went with Leif on his voyage to Vinland. Finn Magnusen says that the error arose from a change of one letter in a pair of short words. See *Grönland's Historiske Mindesmærker*, vol. I, p. 471.

was riding, stumbled, and he fell from his horse[1] and hurt his foot. "It is destined," said Eric, "that I should never discover more lands than this of Greenland, on which we live; and now we must not run hastily into this adventure."[2] Eric accordingly returned home to Brattahlid, but Leif, with his comrades, in all thirty-five men, rigged out their vessel. There was a man from the south country called Tyrker,[3] with the expedition. [A. D. 1000.] They put the ship in order, and put to sea when they were ready. They first came to the land which Biarne had last discovered, sailed up to it, cast anchor, put out a boat and went on shore; but there was no grass to be seen. There were large snowy mountains[4] up the country; but all the way from the sea up to these snowy ridges, the land was one field of snow, and it appeared to them a country of no advantages. Leif said: "It shall not be said of us, as it was of Biarne, that we did not come upon the land; for I will give the country a name, and call it Helluland.[5] Then they went on board again and put to sea, and found another land. They sailed in towards it, put out a boat,

---

[1] Horses could be kept in Greenland now, only with much expense. It appears that anciently it was not so. Undoubtedly there has been more or less of change in climate. Geologists find evidence that at one period, a highly tropical climate must have existed in the northern regions.

[2] Superstition was the bane of the Northman's life. He was also a firm believer in Fate. The doctrines of Fate held the finest Northern minds in a vice-like grasp, so that in many cases their lives were continually overshadowed by a great sorrow. One of the saddest illustrations of this belief, may be found in the *Saga of Grettir the Strong* (given in Baring-Gould's work on Iceland), a Saga in which the doctrine appears with a power that is well nigh appalling.

[3] Some suppose that he was a German, others claim that he was a Turk, as his name might indicate.

[4] Snowy mountains, *Jöklar miklir*, such as Chappell mentions having been seen on the coast, June 14, 1818.

[5] Helluland, from *Hella*, a flat stone, an abundance of which may be found in Labrador and the region round about.

and landed. The country was flat,[1] and overgrown with wood; and the strand far around, consisted of a white sand, and low towards the sea. Then Leif said : " We shall give this land a name according to its kind, and called it Markland."[2] Then they hastened on board, and put to sea again with the wind from the northeast, and were out for two days and made land. They sailed towards it, and came to an island[3] which lay on the north side

---

[1] This agrees with the general features of the country. The *North American Pilot* describes the land around Halifax, as " low in general, and not visible twenty miles off; except from the quarter-deck of a seventy-four. Apostogon hills have a long, level appearance, between Cape Le Have and Port Medway, the coast to the seaward being level and low, and the shores with white rocks and low, barren points; from thence to Shelburne and Port Roseway, are woods. Near Port Haldiman are several barren places, and thence to Cape Sable, which makes the southwest point into Barrington Bay, a low and woody island."— *Antiquitates Americanæ*, p. 423.

[2] Markland is supposed, with great reason, to be Nova Scotia, so well described, both in the Saga, and in the *Coast Pilot*. Markland means woodland. Two days sail thence, brought them in view of Cape Cod, though very likely the sailing time is not correct.

[3] This island has given the interpreters considerable trouble, from the fact that it is said to lie to the northward of the land. And Professor Rafn, in order to identify this island with Nantucket, shows that the north point of the Icelandic compass lay towards the east. But this does not fairly meet the case. There would, perhaps, have been no difficulty in the interpretation, if the Northern Antiquarians had been acquainted with the fact, that in early times an island existed northward from Nantucket, on the opposite coast of Cape Cod. This island, together with a large point of land which now has also disappeared, existed in the times of Gosnold, who sailed around Cape Cod, in 1602. The position of this island, together with the point of land, is delineated in the map given in the Appendix. At one time, some doubt existed in regard to the truthfulness of the accounts, for the reason that those portions of land described, no longer existed. Yet their positions were laid down with scientific accuracy; the outer portion of the island being called Point Care, while the other point was called Point Gilbert. Neither Archer nor Brereton in their accounts of Gosnold's voyage, give the name of the island; but Captain John Smith, in 1614, calls it " Isle Nawset." Smith's *History of Virginia*, vol. II, p. 183. This island was of the drift formation, and as late as half a century ago, a portion of it still

of the land, where they disembarked[1] to wait for good weather. There was dew upon the grass; and having accidentally gotten some of the dew upon their hands and put it in their mouths, they thought that they had never

---

remained, being called Slut Bush. The subject has been very carefully gone into by Mr. Otis, in his pamphlet on the *Discovery of an Ancient Ship on Cape Cod.* Professor Agassiz, writing December 17, 1863, says: "Surprising and perhaps incredible as the statements of Mr. Amos Otis may *appear,* they are nevertheless the direct and natural inference of the observations which may be easily made along the eastern coast of Cape Cod. Having of late felt a special interest in the geological structure of that remarkable region, I have repeatedly visited it during the past summer, and, in company with Mr. Otis, examined, on one occasion, with the most minute care, the evidence of the former existence of Isle Nauset and Point Gilbert. I found it as satisfactory as any geological evidence can be. Besides its scientific interest," he adds, " this result has some historical importance. At all events it fully vindicates Archer's account of the aspect of Cape Cod, at the time of its discovery in 1602, and shows him to have been a truthful and accurate observer." But possibly the vindication may extend back even to the Northmen, whom the learned professor and his colaborers did not have in mind; especially as this discovery will help very materially to explain their descriptions. Now, in the first account of Thorfinn Karlsefne's passage around this part of the Vinland, it is said that they called the shore *Wonder-strand,* " because they were so long going by," Yet any one in sailing past the coast to-day will not be struck with its length. But by glancing at the reconstructed map of Cape Cod (see Appendix), the reader will find that the coast line is greatly increased, so that in order to pass around the cape, the navigator must sail a long distance ; and, comparing this distance travelled with the distance actually gained, the Northmen might well grow weary, and call it Wonder-strand. This quite relieves the difficulty that was felt by Professor Rafn, who labored to show that the island in question was Nantucket, notwithstanding the fact that it lay too far east. For a fuller knowledge of Isle Nauset, see *New England Historic and Genealogical Register,* vol. XVIII, p. 37 ; and *Massachusetts Historical Collections,* vol. VIII, series III, pp. 72-93.

[1] In speaking of the immediate vicinity of *Wonder-strand,* the second account of Thorfinn's expedition says, " There were places without harbors," which has always been the case, this coast being dangerous; yet it is said above that " they landed to wait for good weather." This would be impracticable *now*, except at Chatham ; yet at that day, notwithstanding the absence of harbors, they would find accommodation for their small

tasted anything so sweet as it was.[1] Then they went on board and sailed into a sound [2] that was between the island and a ness [3] that went out northwards from the land, and sailed westward [4] past the ness. There was very shallow [5] water in ebb tide, so that their ship lay dry; and there was a long way between their ship and the water. They were so desirous to get to the land that they would not wait till their ship floated, but ran to the land, to a place where a river comes out of a lake. As soon as their ship was afloat they took the boats, rowed to the ship, towed her

---

vessel somewhere between the island and the mainland. From Bradford's *History*, p. 217, we learn that in 1626-7, there was at this place "a small blind harbore" that "lyes aboute ye middle of Manamoyake Bay," which to-day is filled up by recently formed sandy wastes and salt meadows. This "blind harbore," had at its mouth a treacherous bar of sand. If this harbor had existed in the days of the Northmen, they would not of necessity discover it; and hence while Leif might have landed here and found protection, Thorfinn, in his much larger ship, might have found it needful to anchor, as he appears to have done, in the grounds between Isle Nauset and Point Gilbert, while explorations were being made on the land.

[1] "Honey dew," says Dr. Webb, "occurs in this neighborhood."—*Antiquitates Americanæ*, p. 443.

[2] This sound may have been the water between Point Gilbert and Isle Nauset.

[3] Archer says in his account of Gosnold's voyage: "Twelve leagues from [the end of] Cape Cod, we descried a point [Point Gilbert] with some beach, a good distance off." It is said that the ness, or cape, went out *northward* but we must remember that *eastward* is meant.

[4] This is precisely the course they would steer after doubling that ness or cape which existed in Gosnold's day, and which he named Point Gilbert. The author does not agree with Professor Rafn, in making this point to be at the eastern entrance to Buzzard's bay. If he had known of the existence of the Isle Nauset, he would not have looked for the ness in that neighborhood. At that time Cape Malabar probably did not exist, as we know how rapidly land is formed in that vicinity; yet it would not have attracted notice in comparison with the great broad point mentioned by Archer.

[5] After passing Point Gilbert, shoal water may almost anywhere be found, which appears to have been the case anciently.

up the river,¹ and from thence into the lake,² where they cast anchor, carried their beds out of the ship, and set up their tents. They resolved to put things in order for wintering there, and they erected a large house. They did not want for salmon,³ both in the river and in the lake; and they thought the salmon larger than any they had ever seen before. The country appeared to them of so good a kind, that it would not be necessary to gather fodder for the cattle for winter.⁴ There was no frost in winter,⁵ and the grass was not much withered. Day and night were more equal than in Greenland and Iceland; for on the shortest day the sun was in the sky between Eyktarstad⁶

---

[1] The river was evidently Seaconnet passage and Pocasset river.

[2] This lake is Mount Hope Bay. The writer of the Saga passes over that part of the voyage immediately following doubling of the ness. The tourist in travelling that way by rail will at first take Mount Hope Bay for a lake.

[3] Salmon were formerly so plentiful in this vicinity, that it is said a rule was made, providing that masters should not oblige their apprentices to eat this fish more than twice a week.

[4] It is well known that cattle in that vicinity can pass the winter with little or no shelter, and the sheep on Nantucket, can, when necessary, take care of themselves.

[5] This is an exaggeration, or, possibly, the writer, who was not with the expedition, meant to convey the idea that there was no frost, compared with what was experienced in Greenland and Iceland. The early narrator of the voyage unquestionably tried to make a good impression as regards the climate. In so doing, he has been followed by nearly all who have come after him. Eric the Red told some almost fabulous stories about the climate of Greenland; and yet, because his accounts do not agree with facts, who is so foolish as to deny that he ever saw Greenland? And with as much reason we might deny that Leif came to Vinland. With equal reason, too, we might deny that Morton played the rioter at Merry Mount; for he tells us in his *New English Canaan*, that coughs and colds are unknown in New England. Lieutenant Governor Dudley of Massachusetts complained of these false representations in his day.

[6] This passage was misunderstood by Torfœus, the earliest writer who inquired into these questions, and he was followed by Peringskiold, Malte-Brun and others, who, by their reckoning, made the latitude of Vinland

and the Dagmalastad. Now when they were ready with their house building, [A. D. 1001.] Leif said to his fellow travellers: " Now I will divide the crew into two divisions,

somewhere near Nova Scotia. Yet the recent studies of Rafn and Finn Magnussen, have elucidated the point: " The Northmen divided the heavens or horizons, into eight principal divisions, and the times of the day according to the sun's apparent motion through these divisions, the passage through each of which they supposed to occupy a period of three hours. The day was therefore divided into portions of time corresponding with these eight divisions, each of which was called an *eykt*, signifying an eighth part. This *eykt* was again divided, like each of the grand divisions of the heavens, into two smaller and equal portions, called *stund* or *mal*. In order to determine these divisions of time, the inhabitant of each place carefully observed the diurnal course of the sun, and noted the terrestrial objects over which it seemed to stand. Such an object, whether artificial or natural, was called by the Icelanders, *dagsmark* (daymark). They were also led to make these daymarks by a division of the horizon according to the principal winds, as well as by the wants of their domestic economy The shepherd's rising time, for instance, was called *Hirdis rismál*, which corresponds with half-past four o'clock A. M., and this was the beginning of the natural day of twenty-four hours. Reckoning from *Hirdis rismál* the eight *stund* or eighth half *eykt* ended at just half-past four P. M.; and therefore this particular period was called κατ' ἐξοχήν, EYKT. This *eykt*, strictly speaking, commenced at three o'clock P. M., and ended at half-past four P. M., when it was said to be in *eyktarstadr* or the termination of the *eykt*. The precise moment that the sun appeared in this place indicated the termination of the artificial day (*dagr*), and half the natural day (*dagr*), and was therefore held especially deserving of notice: the hours of labor, also, are supposed to have ended at this time. Six o'clock A. M. was called *midr morgun*; half-past seven A. M., *Dagmal*; nine A. M., *Dagverdarmal*. Winter was considered to commence in Iceland about the seventeenth of October, and Bishop Thorlacius, the calculator of the astronomical calendar, fixes sun-rise in the south of Iceland, on the seventeenth of October, at half past seven A. M. At this hour, according to the Saga, it rose in Vinland on the shortest day, and set at half-past four P. M., which data fix the latitude of the place at 41° 43' 10'', being nearly that of Mount Hope Bay." See *Mem. Antiq. du Nord*, 1836-7, p. 165. Rafn's calculation makes the position 41° 24' 10''. It is based on the view that the observation was made in Vinland when only the upper portion of the disc had appeared above the horizon. The difference, of course, is not important. Thus we know the position of the Icelandic settlement in New England. See *Antiquitates Americanæ*, p. 436.

and explore the country. Half shall stay at home and do the work, and the other half shall search the land; but so that they do not go farther than they can come back in the evening, and that they do not wander from each other." This they continued to do for some time. Leif changed about, sometimes with them, and sometimes with those at home. Leif was a stout and strong man, and of manly appearance; and was, besides, a prudent and sagacious man in all respects.

It happened one evening that a man of the party was missing; and it was the south country man, Tyrker. Leif was very sorry for this, because Tyrker had long been in his father's house, and he loved Tyrker in his childhood. Leif blamed his comrades very much, and proposed to go with twelve men on an expedition to find him ; but they had gone only a short way from the station when Tyrker came to meet them, and he was joyfully received. Leif soon perceived that his foster father [1] was quite

---

[1] In those turbulent times children were not brought up at home, but were sent to be trained up in the families of trusty friends. This was done to preserve the family line. Often, in some bloody feud, a whole household would be destroyed ; yet the children being out at foster, would be preserved, and in due time come to represent the family. In Leif's day, heathenism and lawlessness were on the decline. We have a true picture given us by Dasent, of the way in which children were treated in the heathen age.

He says: "With us, an old house can stand upon a crooked, as well as upon a straight support. But in Iceland, in the tenth century, as in all the branches of that great family, it was only healthy children that were allowed to live. The deformed, as a burden to themselves, their friends, and to society, were consigned to destruction by exposure to the violence of the elements. This was the father's stern right, and, though the mothers of that age were generally blessed with robust offspring, still the right was often exercised. As soon as it was born, the infant was laid upon the bare ground, and, until the father came and looked at it, heard and saw that it was strong in lung and limb, took it up in his arms, and handed it over to the nurse ; its fate hung in the balance, and life or death

merry.[1] Tyrker had a high forehead, sharp eyes, with a small face, and was little in size, and ugly; but was very dexterous in all feats. Leif said to him, "Why art thou so late, my foster-father? and why didst thou leave thy comrades?" He spoke at first long in German, rolled his eyes and knit his brows; but they could not make out what he was saying. After a while, and some delay, he said in Norse, "I did not go much further than they; and yet I have something altogether new to relate, for I found vines and grapes."[2] "Is that true, my foster-father?" said Leif. "Yes, true it is," answered he, "for I was born where

---

depended upon the sentence of its sire. That danger over, it was duly washed, signed with the Thunderer's [Thor's] holy hammer — the symbol of all manliness and strength — and solemnly received into the family as the faithful champion of the ancient gods. When it came to be named, there was what we should call the christening ale. There was saddling, mounting and riding among kith and kin. Cousins came in bands from all points of the compass: dependents, freedmen and thralls all mustered strong. The ale is broached, the board is set, and the benches are thronged with guests; the mirth and revelry are at the highest, when in strides into the hall, a being of awful power, in whom that simple age set full faith. This was the Norne, the wandering prophetess, sybil, fortune teller, a woman to whom it was given to know the weirds of men, and who had come to do honor to the child, and tell his fortune. . . . . After the child was named, he was often put out to foster with some neighbor, his father's inferior in power, and there he grew up with the children of the house, and contracted those friendships and affections which were reckoned better and more binding than the ties of blood."—*Antiquaires du Nord*, 1859, pp. 8–9.

[1] There is nothing in this to indicate that Tyrker was intoxicated, as some have absurdly supposed. In this far off land he found grapes, which powerfully reminded him of his native country, and the association of ideas is so strong, that when he first meets Leif, he breaks out in the language of his childhood, and, like ordinary epicures, expresses his joy, which is all the more marked on account of his grotesque appearance. Is not this a stroke of genuine nature, something that a writer, framing the account of a fictitious voyage, would not dream of?

[2] Grapes grow wild almost everywhere on this coast. They may be found on Cape Cod ripening among the scrub oaks, even within the reach of the ocean spray, where the author has often gathered them.

there was no scarcity of grapes." Now they slept all night, and the next morning Leif said to his men, "Now we shall have two occupations to attend to, and day about; namely, to gather grapes or cut vines, and to fell wood in the forest to lade our vessel." And this advice was followed. It is related that their stern boat was filled with grapes, and then a cargo of wood was hewn for the vessel.[1] Towards spring they made ready and sailed away, and Leif gave the country a name from its products, and called it Vinland.[2] They now sailed into the open sea and had a fair wind until they came in sight of Greenland and the lands below the ice mountains.[3] Then a man put in a word and said to Leif, "Why do you steer so close on the wind?" Leif replied: "I mind my helm and tend to other things too; do you notice anything?" They said that they saw nothing remarkable. "I do not know," said Leif, "whether I see a ship or a rock." Then they looked and saw that it was a rock. But he saw so much better than they, that he discovered men upon the rock. "Now I will," said Leif, "that we hold to the wind, that we may come up to them if they should need help; and if they should not be friendly inclined, it is in our power to do as we please and not theirs." Now they sailed under

---

[1] In Peringskiold's *Heimskringla*, which Laing has followed in translating Leif's voyage for his appendix, this statement of the cutting of wood is supplemented by the following statement: "There was also self-sown wheat in the fields, and a tree which is called massur. Of all these they took samples; and some of the trees were so large that they were used in houses." It is thought that the massur wood was a species of maple. Others have declared that it must have been mahogany, and that therefore the account of Leif's discovery is false. They forget that even George Popham, in writing home to his patron from Sagadahoc, in 1607, says that among the productions of the country are "nutmegs and cinnamon." Yet shall we infer from this that Popham never saw New England?

[2] See Adam of Bremen's testimony in the Introduction.

[3] It will be noticed that they were close upon the Greenland coast.

the rock, lowered their sails, cast anchor, and put out another small boat which they had with them. Then Tyrker asked who their leader was. He said his name was Thorer, and said he was a Northman;[1] "But what is your name?" said he. Leif told his name. "Are you the son of Eric the Red of Brattahlid?" he asked. Leif said that was so. "Now I will," said Leif, "take ye and all on board my ship, and as much of the goods as the ship will store." They took up this offer, and sailed away to Ericfiord with the cargo, and from thence to Brattahlid, where they unloaded the ship. Leif offered Thorer and his wife, Gudrid, and three others, lodging with himself, and offered lodging elsewhere for the rest of the people, both of Thorer's crew and his own. Leif took fifteen men from the rock, and thereafter was called, Leif the Lucky. After that time Leif advanced greatly in wealth and consideration. That winter, sickness came among Thorer's people, and he himself, and a great part of his crew, died. The same winter Eric Red died. This expedition to Vinland was much talked of, and Leif's brother, Thorvald, thought that the country had not been explored enough in different places. Then Leif said to Thorvald, "You may go, brother, in my ship to Vinland if you like; but I will first send the ship for the timber which Thorer left upon the rock." And so it was done.

---

[1] They were evidently Norwegian traders who were shipwrecked while approaching the coast and sailing for the Greenland ports.

SECOND NARRATIVE.

The same spring, King Olaf, as said before, sent Gissur[1] and Hialte[2] to Iceland. The king also sent Leif to Greenland to proclaim Christianity there. The king sent with him, a priest, and some other religious men, to baptize the people and teach them the true faith. Leif sailed the same summer to Greenland; he took up out of the ocean, the people of a ship who were on a wreck completely destroyed, and in a perishing condition. And on this same voyage he discovered Vinland the Good,[3] and came at the close of summer to Brattahlid, to his father Eric. After that time the peeple called him, Leif the Fortunate; but his father Eric said that these two things went against one another; that Leif had saved the crew of the ship, and delivered them from death, and that he had [brought] that bad man into Greenland, that is what he called the priest; but after much urging, Eric was baptized,[4] as well as all the people of Greenland.

---

[1] Gissur, called the White, was one of the greatest lawyers of Iceland. We read that "there was a man named Gissur White, he was Teit's son, Kettlebiarne the Old's son, of Mossfell [Iceland]. Bishop Isleif was Gissur's son. Gissur the White kept house at Mossfell, and was a great Chief."— *Saga of Burnt Nial*, vol. I, p. 146.

[2] Hialte was doubtless the same person who entered the swimming match with King Olaf. See Saga of Olaf Tryggvesson.

[3] This is an error, unless the writer means that the voyage to Vinland, afterwards undertaken, was a part of the same general expedition. Leif went to Greenland first, as we have already seen.

[4] These pagans did not always yield even so readily as Eric. Some in Norway became martyrs to the faith of Odin. See *Saga of Olaf Tryggvesson* (*passim*), in vol. I *of Heimskringla*.

THIRD NARRATIVE.

. The same winter, Leif, the son of Eric the Red, was in high favor with King Olaf, and embraced Christianity. But the summer that Gissur went to Iceland, King Olaf sent Leif to Greenland, to proclaim Christianity. He sailed the same summer for Greenland. He found some men in the sea on a wreck, and helped them; the same voyage,[1] he discovered Vinland the Good, and came at harvest time to Greenland. He brought with him a priest and other religious[2] men, and went to live at Brattahlid with his father Eric. He was afterwards called, Leif the Fortunate. But his father Eric said, that these two things were opposed to one another, because Leif had saved the crew of the ship, and brought evil men to Greenland, meaning the priests.

V. THORVALD ERICSON'S EXPEDITION.

The greater portion of this voyage appears to have been performed during two summers, the expedition finally returning to Greenland on account of the death of their leader. The narrative is taken from *Codex Flatöiensis*, as given in *Antiquitates Americanæ*.

Now Thorvald [A. D. 1002.] made ready for his voyage with thirty men, after consulting his brother Leif. They rigged their ship, and put to sea. Nothing is related of this expedition until they came to Vinland, to the booths put up by Leif, where they secured the ship and tackle,

---

[1] See note to foregoing account.
[2] These appear to have been married men or secular clergy.

and remained quietly all winter and lived by fishing. In spring [A. D. 1003.] Thorvald ordered the vessel to be rigged, and that some men should proceed in the long-boat westward along the coast, and explore it during the summer. They thought the country beautiful and well wooded, the distance small between the forest and the sea, and the strand full of white sand. There were also many islands and very shallow water. They found no abode for man or beast, but on an island far towards the west, they found a corn barn constructed of wood. They found no other traces of human work, and came back in autumn to Leif's booths. The following spring, [A. D. 1004.] Thorvald, with his merchant ship, proceeded eastwards, and towards the north along the land.[1] Opposite to a cape[2] they met bad weather, and drove upon the land and broke their keel, and remained there a long time to repair the vessel. Thorvald said to his companions: "We will stick up the keel here upon the ness, and call the place Kialarness," which they did. Then they sailed away eastward along the country, to a point of land,[3] which was everywhere covered with woods. They moored the vessel to the land, laid out gangways to the shore, and Thorvald with all his ship's company, landed. He said, "Here it is beautiful, and I would willingly set up my abode here."

---

[1] This clearly indicates a voyage around Cape Cod.

[2] This cape was evidently, not Point Gilbert, but the terminus of Cape Cod, known as Race Point, a dangerous place for navigation. It would seem that this was the place referred to, for the reason that the next place mentioned is the east shore, meaning the shore near Plymouth, which is readily seen from the end of Cape Cod in a clear day. It was undoubtedly the vicinity of Race Point that they called Kialarness, or Keel Cape.

[3] Here the version in *Antiquitates Americanæ*, p. 42, is followed, instead of Peringskiold, whose version does not mention the point of land. This place is regarded as Point Alderton, below Boston Harbor. Thorvald evidently sailed along the shore to this point, which is the most remarkable on the east coast.

They afterwards went on board, and saw three specks upon the sand within the point, and went to them and found there were three skin boats with three men under each boat. They divided their men and took all of them prisoners, except one man, who escaped with his boat. They killed eight of them, and then went to the point and looked about them. Within this bay they saw several eminences, which they took to be habitations. Then a great drowsiness came upon them and they could not keep themselves awake, but all of them fell asleep. A sudden scream came to them, and they all awoke; and mixed with the scream they thought they heard the words: "Awake, Thorvald, with all thy comrades, if ye will save your lives. Go on board your ship as fast as you can, and leave this land without delay." In the same moment an innumerable multitude, from the interior of the bay, came in skin boats and laid themselves alongside. Then said Thorvald, "We shall put up our war screens[1] along the gunwales and defend ourselves as well as we can, but not use our weapons much against them." They did so accordingly. The Skrællings[2] shot at them for a while, and then fled away as fast as they could. Then Thorvald asked if anyone was wounded, and they said nobody was hurt. He said: "I have a wound under the arm.[3] An arrow flew

---

[1] These screens were made of planks which could be quickly arranged above the bulwarks, thus affording additional protection against arrows and stones.

[2] These people are sometimes called Smællingar, or small men. Others deduce their name from *skræla*, to dry, alluding to their shriveled aspect; and others from *skrækia* to *shout*. It is evident from the accounts of Egede and Crantz, that they formerly inhabited this part of the country, but were gradually obliged to go northward. It is well known that in other parts of America, these migrations were common. And these people were more likely to take a refuge in Greenland than the Northmen themselves.

[3] The conduct of Thorvald indicates magnanimity of character, thinking first of his men, and afterwards of himself.

between the gunwale and the shield under my arm: here is the arrow, and it will be my death wound. Now I advise you to make ready with all speed to return; but ye shall carry me to the point which I thought would be so convenient for a dwelling. It may be that it was true what I said, that here would I dwell for a while. Ye shall bury me there, and place a cross at my head and one at my feet, and call the place Crossness." Christianity had been established in Greenland at this time;[1] but Eric Red was dead[2] before Christianity was introduced. Now Thorvald died, and they did everything as he had ordered. Then they went away in search of their fellow voyagers; and they related to each other all the news. They remained in their dwelling all winter, and gathered vines and grapes, and put them on board their ships. Towards spring, they prepared to return to Greenland, where they arrived with their vessel, and landed at Ericsfiord, bringing heavy tidings to Leif.

---

[1] Christianity was introduced by Leif, Thorvald's brother, in 1001-2.

[2] This is evidently an error, for Christianity was introduced by Leif, *before* he sailed on his voyage to Vinland. Errors like this abound in all early annals, and why should the Icelandic chronicles be free from them? Every such case will be impartially pointed out. The treatment of this passage by Smith, in his *Dialogues on the Northmen*, p. 127, is far from being candid. He translates the passage thus: "But Eric the Red had died without professing Christianity," and refers the English reader to the Saga of Thorfinn Karlsefne, *Antiquitates Americanæ*, pp. 119-20, as if he would there find a reason for his rendering of the text, which is unequivocal, and is translated literally above. On turning to the authority in question, we find nothing more said than that "Eric was slow to give up his [pagan] religion," and that the affair caused a separation between him and his wife. That he was *slow* to give up his pagan belief, would seem to indicate that he *did* give it up eventually. Moreover, we have the direct statement that he was baptized. Second Narrative of Leif, p. 38.

VI. THORSTEIN ERICSON'S ATTEMPT TO FIND VINLAND.

This version is from *Codex Flatöiensis*, and is given in *Antiquitates Americanæ*, pp. 47–55. The expedition was wholly unsuccessful, and the leader finally died without reaching the desired land. One cannot help feeling, notwithstanding the marvellous events recorded, that the basis of this account, is formed of solid fact. The main narrative is not one likely to have been invented by an impostor.

In the meantime it had happened in Greenland, that Thorstein of Ericsfiord had married, and taken to wife, [A. D. 1005.] Gudrid, the daughter of Thorbiorn, who had been married, as before related, to Thorer, the Eastman.[1] Thorstein Ericsson bethought him now, that he would go to Vinland, for his brother Thorvald's body. He rigged out the same vessel, and chose an able and stout crew. He had with him, twenty-five men, and his wife Gudrid; and as soon as they were ready he put to sea, and they quickly lost sight of the land. They drove about on the ocean the whole summer, without knowing where they were; and in the first week of winter,[2] they landed at Lysifiord in Greenland, in the western settlement. Thorstein looked for lodgings for his men, and got his whole ship's crew accommodated, but not himself and wife; so that for some nights they had to sleep on board. At that time Christianity was but recent in Greenland. One day, early in the morning, some men came to their tent, and the leader asked them what people were in the

---

[1] Norway lay east of Iceland, and hence the people of that country were sometimes called Eastmen.
[2] Winter began October 17. See p. 32, note 6.

tent? Thorstein replies, "Two; who is it that asks?" "Thorstein," was the reply, "and I am called Thorstein the Black, and it is my errand here, to offer thee and thy wife lodging beside me." Thorstein said he would speak to his wife about it; and as she gave her consent, he agreed to it. "Then I shall come for you to-morrow with my horses,[1] for I do not want means to entertain you; but few care to live in my house, for I and my wife live lonely, and I am very melancholy. I have also a different religion[2] from yours, although I think the one you have, the best." Now the following morning he came for them with horses; and they took up their abode with Thorstein Black, who was very friendly towards them. Gudrid had a good outward appearance, and was knowing, and understood well how to behave with strangers. Early in the winter, a sickness prevailed among Thorstein Ericsson's people, and many of his ship men died. He ordered that coffins should be made for the bodies of the dead, and that they should be brought on board, and stowed away carefully; for he said, "I will transport all the bodies to Ericsfiord in summer." It was not long before sickness broke out in Thorstein Black's house, and his wife, who was called Grimhild, fell sick first. She was very stout, and as strong as a man, but yet she could not bear up against the illness. Soon after, Thorstein Ericksson also fell sick, and they both lay ill in bed at the same time; but Grimhild, Thorstein Black's wife died first. When she was dead, Thorstein went out of the room for a skin to lay over the corpse. Then Gudrid said, "My dear Thorstein, be not long away;" which he promised. Then said Thorstein Ericsson, "Our housewife is wonderful, for she

---

[1] They probably had diminutive horses in Greenland, like this of Iceland to-day.

[2] Thorstein Black was a pagan, who nevertheless saw the superior value of the new faith.

raises herself up with her elbows, moves herself forward over the bed-frame, and is feeling for her shoes." In the same moment, Thorstein the Goodman, came back, and instantly, Grimhild laid herself down, so that it made every beam that was in the house, crack. Thorstein now made a coffin for Grimhild's corpse, removed it outside, and buried it. He was a stout and strong man, but it required all his strength to remove the corpse from the house. Now Thorstein Ericsson's illness increased upon him, and he died, which Gudrid his wife took with great grief. They were all in the room, and Gudrid had set herself upon a stool before the bench on which her husband Thorstein's body lay. Now Thorstein the goodman took Gudrid from the stool in his arms, and set himself with her upon a bench just opposite to Thorstein's body,[1] and spoke much with her. He consoled her, and promised to go with her in summer to Ericsfiord, with her husband Thorstein's corpse, and those of his crew. "And," said he, "I shall take with me many servants to console and assist." She thanked him for this. Thorstein Ericsson then raised himself up and said, "Where is Gudrid?" And thrice he said this; but she was silent. Then she said to Thorstein the Goodman, "Shall I give answer or not?" He told her not to answer. Then went Thorstein the Goodman across the room, and sat down in a chair, and Gudrid set herself on his knee; and Thorstein the Goodman said: "What wilt thou make known?" After a while the corpse replies, "I wish to tell Gudrid her fate beforehand, that she may be the better able to bear my death; for I have come to a blessed resting place. And this I have now to tell thee, Gudrid, that thou wilt be married

---

[1] We must here remember the simplicity of manners, which then (as now) prevailed among the Icelanders. The tourist in Iceland is always surprised by the absence of all prudery.

to an Iceland man, and ye will live long together; and from you will descend many men, brave, gallant and wise, and a well pleasing race of posterity. Ye shall go from Greenland to Norway, and from thence to Iceland, where ye shall dwell. And long will ye live together, but thou wilt survive him; and then thou shalt go abroad, and go southwards, and shall return to thy home in Iceland. And there must a church be built, and thou must remain there and be consecrated a nun, and there end thy days."[1] And

---

[1] Whoever inclines to dismiss this whole narrative as an idle fiction, must remember that all history is more or less pervaded by similar stories. The Rev. Cotton, Mather, in his *Magnalia of New England*, gives the account of a great number of supernatural events of no better character than this related in the Saga. Some are ludicrous in the extreme, and others are horrible, both in their inception and end. Among other stories, is that of Mr. Philip Smith, deacon of the church at Hadley, Mass., and a member of the General Court, who appears to have been bewitched. He was finally obliged to keep his bed. Then it is said that the people " beheld fire sometimes on the bed; and when the beholders began to discourse of it, it vanished away. Divers people actually felt something often stir in the bed, at a considerable distance from the man; it seemed as big as a cat, but they could never grasp it. Several trying to lean on the bed's head, tho' the sick man lay wholly still, the bed would shake so as to knock their heads uncomfortably. A very strong man could not lift the sick man, to make him lie more easily, tho' he apply'd his utmost strength unto it; and yet he could go presently and lift the bedstead and a bed, and a man lying on it, without any strain to himself at all. Mr. Smith dies.... After the *opinion* of all had *pronounc'd* him dead, his countenance continued as lively as though he had been alive.... Divers noises were heard in the room where the corpse lay; as the clattering of chairs and stools, whereof no account could be given."—*Magnalia*, ed. 1853, vol. I, p. 455. The account is vouched for by the author, who was one of the most learned divines of his day. Another is given, among the multitude of which he had the most convincing proof. He writes: " It was on the second day of May, in the year 1687, that a most ingenious, accomplish'd and well-dispos'd young gentleman, Mr. Joseph Beacon by Name, about 5 o'clock in the morning, as he lay, whether sleeping or waking he could not say (but he judged the latter of them), had a view of his brother, then at London, although he was himself at our Boston, distanc'd from him a thousand leagues. This his brother appear'd to him in the morning (I say) about 5 o'clock, at Boston, hav-

then Thorstein sank backwards, and his corpse was put in order and carried to the ship. Thorstein the Goodman did all that he had promised. He sold in spring [A. D. 1006.] his land and cattle, and went with Gudrid and all her goods; made ready the ship, got men for it, and then went to Ericsfiord. The body was buried at the church.[1] Gudrid went to Leif's at Brattahlid, and Thorstein the Black took his abode in Ericsfiord, and dwelt there as long as he lived; and was reckoned an able man.

---

ing on him a Bengale gown, which he usually wore, with a napkin ty'd about his head; his *countenance* was very pale, ghastly, deadly, and he had a bloody wound on the side of his forhead. 'Brother,' says the affrighted Joseph, 'Brother,' answered the apparition. Said Joseph, 'What's the matter Brother? how came you here?' The apparition replied: 'Brother I have been most barbarously and inhumanly murdered by a debauch'd fellow, to whom I never did any wrong in my life.' Whereupon he gave a particular description of the murderer; adding, 'Brother, this fellow, changing his name, is attempting to come over to New England, in *Foy* or *Wild:* I would pray you on the arrival of either of these, to get an order from the governour to seize the person whom I now have describ'd, and then do you indict him for the murder of your brother.' And so he vanished." Mather then adds an account, which shows that Beacon's brother was actually murdered as described, dying within the very hour in which his apparition appeared in Boston. He says that the murderer was tried, but, with the aid of his friends, saved his life. Joseph himself, our author says, died "a pious and hopeful death," and gave him the account written and signed with his own hand. And now, while New England history abounds with stories like this, men incline to question an Icelandic writer, because he occasionally indulges in fancies of the same sort. Rather should we look for them, as authentic contemporary signs.

[1] Thorhild's Church. See *Antiquitates Americanæ*, p. 119.

VII. THORFINN KARLSEFNE'S EXPEDITION TO VINLAND.

This was in many respects the most important expedition to New England, both as regards the numbers engaged, and the information and experienced derived. We have three different accounts of this expedition. The first is from the somewhat lengthy Saga of Thorfinn Karlsefne, from the *Arnæ-Magnæan Collection;* the second is from the Saga of Eric the Red, being called "The Account of Thorfinn:" while the third is a briefer relation from *Codex Flatöiensis*. The two first may be found in Rafn's *Antiquitates Americanæ,* pp. 75-200; while the last is also given in the same work, on pp. 55-64.

The Saga of Karlsefne is occupied largely at the beginning with accounts of various matters connected with social life; yet, as such subjects are not essential to the treatment of the subject, they are all omitted, except the account of Thorfinn's marriage with the widow of Thorstein Ericson.

The notes to the narrative of Leif's expedition, which precedes this in the chronological order, supersede the necessity of treating a number of important points suggested again in the present narrative.

It is believed that the principal manuscript of Thorstein Karlsefne is a genuine autograph by one of his descendants, the celebrated Hauk Erlander, the Governor or Lagman of Iceland, in 1295, who was also one of the compilers of the *Landnama-bok*. Erlander was the ninth in descent from Thorfinn. Torfæus, who supposed that this manuscript was lost, knew it only through corrupt extracts in the collection of Biörn Johnson.

There will be found a substantial agreement between the different accounts, notwithstanding they are not the work of eye witnesses. The differences are evidently such, as would not appear in the case of three writers who had banded together for the purpose of carrying out a historical fraud. The Saga of Thorfinn was written in Iceland, while that of Eric was composed in Greenland. The account from the *Flatö Manuscript*, was, of course, written in the island which bears that name, and is extremely brief, wanting many essential particulars.

NARRATIVE OF THORFINN KARLSEFNE.

There was a man named Thord, who dwelt at Höfda, in Höfda-Strand. He married Fridgerda, daughter of Thorer the Idle, and of Fridgerda the daughter of Kiarval, King of the Irish. Thord was the son of Biarne Byrdusmjör,[1] son of Thorvald, son of Aslak, son of Biarne Ironsides, son of Ragnar Lodbrok. They had a son named Snorre, who married Thorhild the Partridge, daughter of Thord Geller. They had a son named Thord Horsehead. Thorfinn Karlsefne was his son, whose mother's name was Thoruna. Thorfinn occupied his time in merchant voyages, and was thought a good trader. One summer he fitted out his ship for a voyage to Greenland, attended by Snorre Thorbrandson of Alptafiord, and a crew of forty men. There was a man named Biarne Grimolfson of Breidafiord, and another named Thorhall Gamlason of Austfiord. The men fitted out a ship at the same time, to voyage to Greenland. They also had a crew of forty men. This ship, and that of Thorfinn, as soon as they were ready, put to sea. It is not said how long they were on the voyage; it is only told that both ships arrived at Erics-

---

[1] Literally, Biarne *Butter-tub*, from which we may, perhaps, infer his personal peculiarity.

fiord in the autumn of that year. Leif[1] and other people rode down to the ships, and friendly exchanges were made. The captains requested Leif to take whatever he desired of their goods. Leif in return, entertained them well, and invited the principal men of both ships to spend the winter with him at Brattahlid. The merchants accepted his invitation with thanks. Afterwards their goods were moved to Brattahlid, where they had every entertainment that they could desire; therefore their winter quarters pleased them much. When the Yule feast began, Leif was silent and more depressed than usual. Then Karlsefne said to Leif: "Are you sick friend Leif? you do not seem to be in your usual spirits. You have entertained us most liberally, for which we desire to render you all the service in our power. Tell me what it is that ails you." "You have received what I have been able to offer you," said Leif, "in the kindest manner and there is no idea in my mind that you have been wanting in courtesy; but I am afraid lest when you go away, it may be said that you never saw a Yule[2] feast so meanly celebrated as that which draws near, at which you will be entertained by Leif of Brattahlid." "What shall never be the case, friend," said Karlsefne, "we have ample stores in the ship; take of these what you wish, and make a feast as splendid as you please." Leif accepted this offer, and the Yule

---

[1] Throughout this narrative of Thorfinn, the name of Eric occurs where that of Leif should be given. Eric died five years before Thorfinn came over to Greenland. This account having been written in Iceland, the author made a very natural mistake in supposing that Eric was still at the head of the family. The proper change has been made in the translation, to avoid confusion.

[2] *Yule* was a pagan festival, held originally in honor of Thor, the god of War, at the beginning of February, which was the opening of the Northman's year. But as Christianity had been established in Greenland for five years, the festival was now probably changed to December, and held in honor of Christ.

began; and so well were Leif's plans made, that all were surprised that such a rich feast could be prepared in so poor a country. After the Yule feast, Karlsefne began to treat with Leif, as to the marriage of Gudrid,[1] Leif being the person to whom the right of betrothal belonged. Lief gave a favorable reply, and said she must fulfill that destiny which fate had assigned, and that he had heard of none except a good report of him; and in the end it turned out that Karlsefne married Gudrid, and their wedding was held at Brattahlid, this same winter.

[A. D. 1007.] The conversation often turned at Brattahlid, on the discovery of Vinland the Good, and they said that a voyage there had great hope of gain. And after this Karlsefne and Snorre made ready for going on a voyage there, the following spring. Biarne and Thorhall Gamlason, before mentioned, joined him with a ship. There was a man named Thorvard, who married Freydis, natural daughter of Eric Red, and he decided to go with them, as did also Thorvald, son [2] of Eric. And Thorhall, commonly called the Hunter, who had been the huntsman of Eric in the summer, and his steward in the winter, also went. This Thorhall was a man of immense size and of great strength, and dark complexion and taciturn, and when he spoke, it was always jestingly. He was always inclined to give Leif evil advice, and was an enemy of Christianity. He knew much about desert lands; and was in the same

---

[1] Widow of Thorstein Ericson. Rafn thinks, as she is mentioned in this Saga by two names, Gudrid and Thurid, that one was her name in childhood, and the other in her maturer years, when Christianity came to have a practical bearing. Her father's name was Thorbiorn, derived from Thor. It was supposed that those who bore the names of gods would find in these names a charm or special protection from danger.

[2] This is a mistake, Eric's son was dead. It must have been another Thorvald.

ship with Thorvord and Thorvald. These used the ship which brought Thorbiorn from Iceland. There were in all, forty men and a hundred.[1] They sailed to the West district [of Greenland], and thence to Biarney;[2] hence they sailed south a night and a day. Then land was seen, and they launched a boat and explored the land; they found great flat stones, many of which were twelve ells broad. There were a great number of foxes there. They called the land Helluland.[3] Then they sailed a day and a night in a southerly course, and came to a land covered with woods, in which there were many wild animals. Beyond this land to the southeast, lay an island on which they slew a bear. They called the island Bear island,[4] and the land, Markland. Thence they sailed south two days and came to a cape. The land lay on the right [starboard] side of the ship, and there were long shores of sand. They came to land, and found on the cape, the keel of a ship, from which they called the place Kiarlarness,[5] and the

---

[1] The Northmen had two ways of reckoning a hundred, the short and the long. The long hundred was a hundred and twenty. We read in Tegner's *Frithiof's Saga*:

> "But a house for itself was the banquet hall, fashioned in fir wood;
> Not five hundred, though told *ten dozen* to every hundred,
> Filled that chamber so vast, when they gathered for Yule-tide carousing."
> *American ed.*, chap. III, p. 13.

Professor Rafn infers that the long hundred was here meant, because he thinks that the inscription on Dighton Rock indicates CLI., the number of men Karlsefne had with him, after losing nine.

[2] The present island of Disco, also called by the Northmen, Biarney, or Bear island.

[3] The northern coast of America was called Helluland the Great, and Newfoundland, Helluland, or Little Helluland.—*Antiquitates Americanæ*, p. 419.

[4] Supposed from the distance to be the Isle of Sable.

[5] Leif had left the keel of his vessel here on the point of this cape, which was Cape Cod. In calling it by this name, they simply followed his example.

shores they also called Wonder-strand, because it seemed so long sailing by. Then the land became indented with coves, and they ran the ship into a bay,[1] whither they directed their course. King Olaf Tryggvesson had given Leif two Scots,[2] a man named Haki and a woman named Hekia; they were swifter of foot than wild animals. These were in Karlfsefne's ship. And when they had passed beyond Wonder-strand, they put these Scots ashore, and told them to run over the land to the southwest, three days, and discover the nature of the land, and then return. They had a kind of garment that they called kiafal, that was so made that a hat was on top, and it was open at the sides, and no arms; fastened between the legs with a button and strap, otherwise they were naked. When they returned, one had in his hand a bunch of

---

[1] This bay was the bay then situated between Point Gilbert and Isle Nauset, which Professor Agassiz proves to have existed. The writers do not mention this island in either of the accounts of Thorfinn's voyage; but it has been shown that Isle Nauset lay close to the shore, so that they would not know that it *was* an island without particular examination; and if they were aware of its existence, it was not necessary to speak of it. Leif landed upon it, therefore it was mentioned by the author who wrote the account of his voyage. Yet Thorfinn's chroniclers help to prove its existence, by showing that beyond Wonder-strand there was a bay where they could safely ride at anchor for three days.

It must be noticed that the events are not set down in their exact order, for after the writer gets the vessels into the bay, he goes back to speak of the landing of the Scots. Gosnold anchored in this same place in the night, and in the morning he remarked the number of coves, or as he calls them "breaches," in the land. The Saga mentions the same thing, saying that the land "became indented with coves." These coves have now disappeared, yet the testimony of Gosnold shows how accurately the Northmen observed this part of the coast. Like Gosnold, they found it convenient and safe to lie here for a while.

[2] This is the first time we hear of slaves being brought into Vinland. We have already seen that with the proud Northman, slavery was a reality. One of the near relatives of Ingolf, the first Northman who settled in Iceland, was murdered by his Scotch (Irish) slaves.

grapes, and the other an ear of corn. They went on board, and afterwards the course was obstructed by another bay.[1] Beyond this bay was an island,[2] on each side of which was a rapid current, that they called the Isle of Currents.[3] There was so great a number of eider ducks[4] there, that they could hardly step without treading on their eggs. They called this place Stream Bay.[5] Here they brought their ships to land, and prepared to stay. They had with them all kinds of cattle. The situation of the place[6] was pleasant, but they did not care for anything, except to explore the land. Here they wintered without sufficient food. The next summer [A. D. 1008.] failing to catch fish, they began to want food. Then Thorhall the Hunter disappeared.

They found Thorhall, whom they sought three days, on the top of a rock, where he lay breathing, blowing through his nose and mouth, and muttering. They asked why he had gone there. He replied that this was nothing that concerned them.[7] They said that he should go home with them, which he did. Afterwards a whale was cast ashore[8] in that place; and they assembled and cut it up, not

---

[1] This was Nantucket or Martha's Vineyard, then probably united, forming one island.

[2] Nantucket island, which then was probably united with Martha's Vineyard.

[3] *Straumey*, or Straum Isle, which, perhaps, indicates their knowledge of the Gulf stream.

[4] The gull, or some similar bird is here referred to.

[5] Buzzards Bay. The general positions are fixed by the astronomical calculations from the data given in Leif's voyage. See note to p. 33.

[6] The shore opposite Martha's Vineyard.

[7] It would appear from what follows that he was engaged in a heathen invocation. This is the only instance on record of honor being paid to this heathen god on the shores of New England, yet we unwittingly recognize him every time we say Thursday, that is, Thor's Day.

[8] In olden times a certain portion of every whale cast ashore on Cape Cod, formed a perquisite of the clergy.

knowing what kind of a whale it was. They boiled it with water, and devoured it, and were taken sick. Then Thorhall said: "Now you see that Thor[1] is more prompt to give aid than your Christ. This was cast ashore as a reward for the hymn which I composed to my patron Thor, who rarely forsakes me." When they knew this, they cast all the remains of the whale into the sea, and commended their affairs to God. After which the air became milder, and opportunities were given for fishing; and from that time there was an abundance of food; and there were beasts on the land, eggs in the island, and fish in the sea.

They say that Thorhall desired to go northward around Wonder-strand to explore Vinland, but Karlsefne wished to go along the shore south. Then Thorhall prepared himself at the island, but did not have more than nine men in his whole company, and all the others went in the company of Karlsefne. When Thorhall was carrying water to his ship, he sang this verse:

> "People said when hither I
> Came, that I the best

---

[1] Literally the Red-beard, as Thor is supposed to have had a beard of that color. The principal deity of the Northmen was Odin, a king who died in his bed in Sweden, and was afterwards apotheosized. He was called the "Terrible god." The souls of men slain in battle were received by him into the hall of the gods. Next was Frigga or Frey, his wife, considered the goddess of earth and mother of the gods. She finally fell into the place occupied by the classic Venus. Next was Thor the Red-beard, synonymous with Jupiter. These three composed the supreme council of the gods. Afterwards came the good and gentle Balder, the Northman's Christ; then came Brage, patron of eloquence and poetry, and his wife Iduna, charged with the care of certain apples, with Heimdal the porter of the gods and builder of the rainbow, and Loke, a kind of Satan or evil principle, aided by his children, the Wolf Fenris, the Serpent Midgard, and Hela, or Death.

> Drink would have, but the land
> It justly becomes me to blame;
> I, a warrior, am now obliged
> To bear the pail;
> Wine touches not my lips,
> But I bow down to the spring."

And when they had made ready and were about to sail, Thorhall sang:

> "Let us return
> Thither where [our] country-men rejoice,
> Let the ship try
> The smooth ways of the sea;
> While the strong heroes
> Live on Wonder-strand
> And there boil whales
> Which is an honor to the land."

Afterwards he sailed north to go around Wonder-strand and Kiarlarness, but when he wished to sail westward, they were met by a storm from the west and driven to Ireland, where they were beaten and made slaves. And, as merchants [1] reported, there Thorhall died.

It is said that Karlsefne, with Snorre and Biarne and his comrades, sailed along the coast south. They sailed long until they came to a river flowing out from the land through a lake into the sea, where there were sandy shoals, where it was impossible to pass up, except with the highest tide. Karlsefne sailed up to the mouth of the river with his folk, and called the place Hop.[2] Having

---

[1] We shall see from another part of this work, that the trade at that period between Ireland and Iceland, was very large.

[2] This corresponds precisely to Mount Hope bay. The Taunton river runs through it, and thence flows to the sea by Pocasset river and Seaconnet passage. Hop is from the Icelandic *I Hópi*, to recede, hence to form a bay. The coincidence in the names is striking.

come to the land, they saw that where the ground was low corn[1] grew, and where it was higher, vines were found. Every river was full of fish.

They dug pits where the land began, and where the land was highest; and when the tide went down, there were sacred fish[2] in the pits. There were a great number of all kinds of wild beasts in the woods. They stayed there half a month and enjoyed themselves, and did not notice anything; they had their cattle with them. And early one morning, when they looked around, they saw a great many skin boats, and poles were swung upon them, and it sounded like reeds shaken by the wind, and they pointed to the sun. Then said Karlsefne, "What may this mean?" Snorre Thorbrandson replied, "It may be that this is a sign of peace, so let us take a white shield and hold it towards them." They did so. Thereupon they rowed towards them, wondering at them, and came to land. These people were swarthy and fierce, and had bushy hair on their heads; they had very large eyes and broad cheeks. They stayed there for a time, and gazed upon those they met, and afterwards rowed away southward around the ness.

Karlsefne and his people had made their houses above the lake, and some of the houses were near the lake, and others more distant. They wintered there, and there was no snow, and all their cattle fed themselves on the grass.[3]

---

[1] Perhaps wheat. *Sialfsana hveitiakrar.*

[2] In Iceland the halibut is called the sacred fish. Pliny uses the same name, which indicates that the water is safe where they were found. The halibut and most of the flat fish, such as flounders, are plentiful in that vicinity. The flounders are easily taken, and those who know how, often find them in very shoal water, burrowing just under the surface of the sand like the king crab.

[3] This is language that might be employed by an Icelander, to indicate the difference between the new country and his own. It may have been an intentional exaggeration, similar to those of Eric in describing Greenland. Yet even if it were a serious attempt at history, it could not be

But when spring came [A. D. 1009.] they saw one morning early, that a number of canoes rowed from the south round the ness; so many, as if the sea were sown with coal; poles were also swung on each boat. Karlsefne and his people then raised up the shield, and when they came together they began to trade; and these people would rather have red cloth; for this they offered skins and real furs. They would also buy swords and spears, but this, Karlsefne and Snorre forbade. For a whole fur skin, the Skrællings took a piece of red cloth, a span long, and bound it round their heads. Thus went on their traffic for a time; then the cloth began to be scarce with Karlsefne and his people, and they cut it up into small pieces, which were not wider than a finger's breath, and yet the Skrællings gave just as much as before, and more.

It happened that a bull, which Karlsefne had, ran out of the wood and roared aloud; this frightened the Skrællings, and they rushed to their canoes and rowed away toward the south; and after that they were not seen for three whole weeks. But at the end of that time, a great number of Skrælling's ships were seen coming from the south like a rushing torrent, all the poles turned from the sun, and they all yelled very loud. Then Karlsefne's people took a red[1] shield and held it towards them. The Skrællings leaped out of their vessels, and after this, they went against each other and fought. There was a hot shower of weapons, because the Skrællings had slings. Karlsefne's people saw that they raised up on a pole, a very large ball, something like a sheep's paunch, and of a blue color; this they swung from the pole over Karlsefne's men, upon

---

regarded as farther from the truth, than Dr. Cotton Mather's description of the climate of New England, where he tells us that water tossed up in the air, came down ice; and that in one place in Massachusetts, it actually snowed wool, some of which, he tells us, he preserved in a box in his study.

[1] The red shield was the sign of war, and the white, of peace.

the ground, and it made a great noise as it fell down.[1] This caused great fear with Karlsefne and his men, so that they only thought of running away, and they retreated along the river, for it seemed to them that the Skrællings pressed them on all sides; they did not stop until they came to some rocks, where they made a bold stand. Freydis came out and saw that Karlsefne's people fell back, and she cried out, "Why do you run, strong men as you are, before these miserable creatures, whom I thought you would knock down like cattle? And if I had arms, methinks I could fight better than any of you." They gave no heed to their words. Freydis would go with them, but she was slower, because she was pregnant; still she followed after them into the woods. She found a dead man in the woods; it was Thorbrand Snorreson, and there stood a flat stone stuck in his head; the sword lay naked by his side. This she took up, and made ready to defend herself. Then came the Skrællings toward her; she drew out her breasts from under her clothes, and dashed them against the naked sword;[2] by this the Skrællings became frightened and ran off to their ships, and rowed away. Karlsefne and his men then came up and praised her courage. Two men fell on Karlsefne's side, but a number of the Skrællings. Karlsefne's band was overmatched. And now they went home to their dwellings and bound up their wounds; and considered what crowd that was that pressed upon them from the land side, and it now seemed to them that it could have hardly been real people from the ships, but that these must have been

---

[1] This account can hardly be explained. These people, doubtless, had their own ideas of the best method of conducting a fight. They were evidently Esquimaux, and formerly, according to Crantz, appear to have lived on this coast before it was occupied by the Indians, who, being a superior race, soon drove them away.

[2] This appears childish, yet there is nothing to indicate that it was not so.

optical illusions. The Skrællings also found a dead man, and an axe lay by him; one of them took up the axe and cut wood with it; and then one after another did the same, and thought it was a fine thing and cut well. After that, one took it and cut at a stone, so that the axe broke, and then they thought that it was of no use, because it would not cut stone, and they cast it away.

Karlsefne and his people now thought that they saw, although the land had many good qualities, that they still would always be exposed there to the fear of attacks from the original dwellers.[1] They decided, therefore, to go away, and to return to their own land. They coasted northward along the shore,[2] and found five Skrællings clad in skins, sleeping near the sea. They had with them vessels containing animal marrow, mixed with blood.[3] Karlsefne's people thought that these men had been banished from the land; they killed them. After that they came to a ness, and many wild beasts were there, and the ness was covered all over with dung, from the beasts which had lain there during the night. Now they came back to Straumfiord, and there was a plenty of everything that they wanted to have. [It is thus that some men say, that Biarne and Gudrid stayed behind, and one hundred men with them, and did not go farther; but that Karlsefne and Snorre went southward, and forty men with them, and were not longer in Hop than barely two months, and the same summer came back.][4] Karlsefne then went with one

---

[1] Thorfinn's experience was similar to that of most early colonists in America.

[2] This, very likely, was a short exploration up Narragansett bay.

[3] The ancient Mexicans mixed human blood with bread offered on the altar of their deities.

[4] The lines inclosed in brackets, convey what the writer understood to be a mere rumor. This report was evidently untrue, yet it shows his honest intentions.

ship to seek Thorhall the Hunter, but the rest remained behind, and they sailed northward past Kiarlarness, and thence westward, and the land was upon their larboard hand. There were wild woods over all, as far as they could see, and scarcely any open places. And when they had sailed long a river ran out of the land from east to west. They sailed into the mouth of the river, and lay by its banks.[1]

It chanced one morning that Karlsefne and his people saw opposite in an open place in the woods, a speck which glittered in their sight, and they called out towards it, and it was a Uniped,[2] which thereupon hurried down to the

---

[1] They appear to have sailed around Cape Cod, then steered across to Plymouth, coasted up the shore towards Point Alderton, and entered Scituate harbor, or some other river mouth on that coast.

[2] *Einfoetingr*, from *ein*, one, and *fótr*, foot. This term appears to have been given by some old writers, to one of the African tribes, on account of a peculiarity of dress, which Wormskiold describes as a triangular cloth, hanging down so low, both before and behind, that the feet were concealed. In an old work called *Rimbigla,* a tribe of this class, dwelling in Blaland, Ethiopia, are thus described.—*Beamish's Northmen*, p. 101. We do not say how far the Saga writer employs his fancy on the Uniped, yet he is quite excusable, considering the weakness of modern writers. In 1634, Hans Egede wrote as follows about a hideous monster: "July 6th, a most hideous sea monster was seen, which reared itself so high above the water, that its head overtopped our mainsail..... Instead of fins, it had broad flaps like wings; its body seemed to be overgrown like shell work.... It was shaped like a serpent behind, and when it dived, ... raised its tail above the water, a whole ship's length."—*Egede's Greenland*, p. 85 ; *Crantz's Greenland*, vol. III, p. 116. Hudson even describes a mermaid.

The Rev. Dr. Cotton Mather, who has before been quoted, gives among other notable facts in his *Magnalia,* the statement, that in June, 1682, Mary Hortado, of Salmon Falls, was going with her husband "over the river in her canoe, when they saw the head of a man, and about three foot off, the *tail* of a cat, swimming before the canoe, but no body to join them..... A stone

bank of the river, where they lay. Thorvald Ericson stood at the helm, and the Uniped shot an arrow into his bowels. Thorvald drew out the arrow and said: " It has killed me! To a rich land we have come, but hardly shall we enjoy any benefit from it." Thorvald soon after died [1] of his wound. Upon this the Uniped ran away to the northward; Karlsefne and his people went after him, and saw him now and then, and the last time they saw him, he ran out into a bay. Then they turned back, and a man sang these verses:

> The people chased
> A uniped
> Down to the beach.
> Behold he ran
> Straight over the sea —
> Hear thou, Thorfinn!

They drew off to the northward, and saw the country of the Unipeds; they would not then expose their men any longer. They looked upon the mountain range that was at Hop, and that which they now found,[2] as all one, and it also appeared to be of equal length from Straumfiord to both places. The third winter they were in Straumfiord. They now became much divided by party feeling, and the women were the cause of it, for those who were unmarried would injure those who were married, and hence arose great disturbance. There was born the first autumn, Snorre, Karlsefne's son, and he was three years old when they went away. When they sailed from Vinland they

---

thrown by an invisible hand after this, caus'd a swelling and a soreness in her head: and she was *bitten* on both arms black and blue, and her breast scratch'd. The impression of the teeth, which were like a man's teeth, were seen by many."—*Magnalia*, vol. I, p. 454.

[1] See p. 41. This *may* be a wrong version of the death of the son of Eric.
[2] The Blue Hills, which extend to Mount Hope.

had a south wind, and then came to Markland, and found there, five Skrællings, and one was bearded; two were females, and two boys; they took the boys, but the others escaped, and the Skrællings sank down in the ground.[1] These boys they took with them; they taught them the language, and they were baptized. They called their mother Vathelldi, and their father, Uvæge. They said that two kings ruled over the Skrællings, and that one was named Avalldania, but the other Valldidia. They said that no houses were there; people lay in caves or in holes. They said there was a land on the other side, just opposite their country, where people lived who wore white clothes, and carried poles before them, and to these were fastened flags, and they shouted loud; and the people think that this was White-man's land, or Great Ireland.[2]

Biarne Grimolfson was driven with his ship into the Irish ocean, and they came into a worm sea,[3] and soon the ship began to sink under them. They had a boat which was smeared with sea oil, for the worms do not attack that. They went into the boat, and then saw that it could not hold them all. Then said Biarne: "As the boat will not hold more than half of our men, it is my counsel that lots should be drawn for those to go in the boat, for it shall not be according to rank." This, they all thought so generous an offer, that no one would oppose it. They then did so that lots were drawn, and it fell to Biarne to go in the boat, and the half of the men with him,

---

[1] That is, they fled into their abodes.

[2] The location of this place will be discussed in the Minor Narratives.

[3] This was the teredo, which is often so destructive, and which caused Columbus to abandon a ship at *Puerto Bello,* because he could not keep her afloat. See Irving's *Columbus,* p. 287.

for the boat had not room for more. But when they had gotten into the boat, an Icelandic man that was in the ship, and had come with Biarne from Iceland, said: "Dost thou mean, Biarne, to leave me here?" Biarne said: "So it seems." Then said the other: "Very different was the promise to my father, when I went with thee from Iceland, than thus to leave me, for thou said that we should both share the same fate." Biarne said, "It shall not be thus; go down into the boat, and I will go up into the ship, since I see that thou art so anxious to live."[1] Then Biarne went up into the ship, and this man down into the boat, and after that they went on their voyage, until they came to Dublin, in Ireland, and there told these things; but it is most people's belief that Biarne and his companions were lost in the worm sea, for nothing was heard of them after that time.

THE ACCOUNT OF THORFINN.

That same winter [A. D. 1006-7.] there was much discussion about the affairs of Brattahlid; and they set up the game of chess, and sought amusement in the reciting of history,[2] and in many other things, and were able to pass life joyfully. And Karlsefne and Snorre resolved to seek Vinland, but there was much discussion about it. But it turned out that Karlsefne and Snorre prepared their ships to seek Vinland the following summer. [A. D. 1007.] And in this enterprise Biarne and Thorhall joined as comrades with their own ship and crew, who were their followers. There was a man named Thorvald, a relation[3]

---

[1] This was truly in accordance with the noble spirit of the great Northmen, who had no fear of death, which to heroes, is the shining gate of Valhalla.

[2] This is one evidence that history was cultivated in Greenland.

[3] Here the writer is correct. See note 2, p. 51.

of Eric. Thorhall was called the Hunter; he long had
hunted with Eric in summer, and had the care of many
things. Thorhall was of great stature, large and swarthy
face, of a hard nature, taciturn, saying little of affairs, and
nevertheless crafty and malicious, always inclined to evil,
and opposed in his mind to the Christian religion, from its
first introduction into Greenland. Thorhall indulged in
trifling, but nevertheless Eric was used to his familiarity.
He went in the ship with Thorvald, and was well acquainted with uninhabitable places. He used the ship in
which Thorbiorn came; and Karlsefne engaged comrades
for the expedition; and the best part of the sailors of
Greenland were with him. They carried in their ships,
forty and a hundred men. Afterwards they sailed to West
bygd and Biarney-isle. They sailed from Biarney-isle
with a north wind, and were on the sea day and night,
when they found land, and sending a boat to the shore,
explored the land, where they found many flat stones of
such great size, that they exceeded in length the size of
two men. There were foxes there. And they gave the
land a name, and called it Helluland. After this, they
sailed a night and a day with a north wind. They came
to a land in which were great woods and many animals.
Southwest, opposite the land, lay an island. Here they
found a bear, and called the island, Bear island. This
land, where there were woods, they called Markland.
After a voyage of a day and a night, they saw land, and
they sailed near the land and saw that it was a cape; they
kept close to the shore with the wind on the starboard side,
and left the land upon the right side of the ship. There
were places without harbors, long shores and sands. When
they went to the shore with a boat, they found the keel of
a ship, and they called the place, Kiarlarness;[1] and they

---

[1] See page 52.

gave the shore a name, and called it Wonder-strand, because they were so long going by. Then another bay extended into the land, and they steered into the bay.[1] When Leif was with King Olaf Tryggvesson, he sent him to establish the Christian religion in Greenland; then the king gave him two Scots-folk, a man named Hake, and a woman named Hekia. The king told Leif to take them with his men, if he would have his commands done quickly, as they were swifter than beasts. These folk, Leif and Eric gave to Karlsefne, as followers. When they were come opposite Wonder-strand, they put the Scots on the shore, and told them to run southward and explore the country, and return before the end of three days. They were thus clothed, having a garment called a Biafal;[2] it was made so that a hat was on top, open at the sides, without arms, buttoned between the legs, and fastened with a button and strap; and the rest was bare.

They came to anchor and lay by, until the three days passed, when they returned, one having in his hand a vine, and the other, self-sown wheat. Karlsefne said that they had found a fruitful land. Afterwards they were received into the ship, and they went on their way until a bay intersected the land. They steered the ship into the bay. On the outside was an island, and there was a great tide around the island. This they called, Straumey.[3] There was a great number of birds, and it was scarcely possible to find a place for their feet among the eggs. Then

---

[1] The same bay referred to in the previous account, and which lay between Point Gilbert and Isle Nauset. Archer, in his account of Gosnold's voyage, says, that when they rounded Point Care, the extremity of Isle Nauset, "We bore up again with the land, and in the night, came with it anchoring in eight fathoms, the ground good." Here it will be seen that the Northmen lay safely for three days.

[2] In the first account it is called a Kiafal.

[3] The agreement with the first account is substantial.

they steered into a long bay which they called Straumfiord, where they landed from their ships and began to prepare habitations. They brought with them all kinds of cattle, and they found sufficient pasturage. There were mountains, and the prospect was pleasant. But they cared for nothing, except to explore the land; there was a great abundance of grass. Here they wintered, and the winter was severe, and they did not have stores laid up, they began to be in want of food, and failed to catch fish. So they sailed over to the island,[1] hoping that they might find means of subsistence, either on what they could catch, or what was cast ashore. But they found but little better fare, though the cattle were better off. [A. D. 1008.] Afterwards they prayed to God, to send them food; which prayer was not answered as soon as desired. Then Thorhall disappeared, and a search was made, which lasted three days. On the morning of the fourth day, Karlsefne and Biarne found him lying on the top of a rock; there he lay stretched out, with open eyes, blowing through his mouth, and muttering to himself. They asked him why he had gone there. He replied that it did not concern them and not to wonder, as he was old enough to take care of himself, without their troubling themselves with his affairs. They asked him to go home with them; this he did. After that a whale was cast up, and they ran down to cut it up; nevertheless they did not know what kind it was. Neither did Karlsefne, though acquainted with whales, know this one. Then the cooks dressed the whale, and they all ate of it, and it made them all sick. Then Thorhall said, "It is clear now that the Red-beard is more prompt to give aid than your Christ. This food is a reward for a hymn which I made to my god Thor, who has seldom deserted me." When they heard this,

---

[1] This was probably Martha's Vineyard.

none would eat any more, and threw what was left from the rock, committing themselves to God. After this the opportunity was given of going after fish, and there was no lack of food. They sailed into Straumfiord, and had abundance of food and hunting on the mainland, with many eggs, and fish from the sea.

And now they began to consider where they should settle next. Thorhall the Hunter wished to go northward around Wonder-strand and Kiarlarness to explore Vinland, but Karlsefne wished to go southwest, thinking likely that there would be larger tracts of country the further they went south. Thorhall made ready at the island, and only nine men went with him, all the rest of the ship folk went with Karlsefne. One day Thorhall was carrying water to his ship; he drank it and sang this verse:

"People promised me when hither I
Came, then the best drink
I should have; but the country
I must denounce to all;
Here you are forced by hand
To bear the pail to the water,
I must bend me down to the spring;
Wine did not come to my lips."

Afterwards they left the land, and Karlsefne went with them to the island. Before they hoisted sail, Thorhall sang these verses:

"Let us return
Home to our countrymen,
Let the vessel try
The broad path of the sea;
While the persevering
Men, who praise the land
Are building, and boil the whales
Here on Wonder-strand."

Thereupon they sailed northward around Wonder-strand and Kialarness. But when they wished to cruise westward, a storm came against them, and drove them to Ireland, where they were beaten and made slaves. There Thorhall passed his life.[1]

Karlsefne, with Snorre and Biarne and the rest of his comrades, sailed south. They sailed long until they came to a river, which flowed from the land through a lake, and passed into the sea. Before the mouth of the river were great islands, and they were not able to enter the river except at the highest tide.[2] Karlsefne sailed into the mouth of the river, and called the land Hop. There they found fields, where the land was low, with wild corn, and where the land was high, were vines. And every river was full of fish. They made pits in the sand, where the tide rose highest, and at low tide, sacred fish were found in these pits, and in the woods was a great number of all kinds of beasts. Here they stayed half a month, enjoying themselves, but observing nothing new. Early one morning, on looking around, they saw nine skin boats, in which were poles that, vibrating towards the sun, gave out a sound like reeds shaken by the wind. Then Karlsefne said: "What, think you, does this mean?" Snorre said: "It is possible that it is a sign of peace; let us raise up a white shield and hold it towards them:" this they did. Then they rowed towards them, wondering at them, and came to land. These men were small of stature and fierce, having a bushy head of hair, and very great eyes and wide cheeks. They remained some time wondering at them, and afterwards rowed southward around the cape. They

---

[1] The first narrative says substantially the same thing, that Thorhall died in Ireland.

[2] The first narrative speaks of the shoals. The islands and shoals both doubtless existed then. Since that time great changes have taken place in the physical aspects of that region.

built dwellings beyond the lake, others made houses near the mainland, and others near the lake. Here they spent the winter. No snow fell,[1] and all their cattle fed under the open sky. They decided to explore all the mountains[2] that were in Hop; which done, they [A. D. 1009.] went and passed the third winter in Straum bay. At this time they had much contention among themselves, and the unmarried women vexed the married. The first autumn, Snorre, Karlsefne's son, was born, and he [was three years old] when they went away. They had a south wind, and came to Markland, and found five Skrællings, of whom one was a man, and two women, and two were boys. Karlsefne took the boys, and the others escaped and sank down into the earth. They carried the boys away with them, and taught them the language, and they were baptized. And the name of their mother was Vatheldi, and their father, Uvæge. They said that two kings ruled over the Skrællinger's land, one was named Avalldania, and the other, Valldidia; that they had no houses, but lived in dens and caves. In another part of the country, there was a region where the people wore white clothes, and shouted loud, and carried poles with flags. This they thought to be White-man's land. After this they came into Greenland, and passed the winter with Leif, son of Eric Red. Biarne Grimolfson was carried out into the Greenland[3] sea, and came into a worm sea, which they did not observe, until their ship was full of worm holes. They considered what should be done. They had a stern boat, smeared with oil; they say that wood covered with oil, the worms will not bore. The result of the council was, that as many should go into the boat as it would hold. It then appeared

---

[1] This might have been the case on some remarkable season.

[2] This range extends to the Blue Hills of Massachusetts, which indicates considerable activity in exploration.

[3] Also called the Irish sea, and the sea before Vinland.

that the boat would not hold more than one-half of the men. Then Biarne ordered that the men should go in the boat by lot, and not according to rank. And as it would not hold all, they accepted the proposition, and when the lots were drawn, the men went out of the ship into the boat. And the lot was that Biarne should go down from the ship to the boat with one-half of the men. Then those to whom the lot fell, went down from the ship to the boat. And when they had come into the boat, a young Icelander, who was the companion of Biarne, said: "Now thus do you intend to leave me, Biarne?" Biarne replied, "That now seems necessary." He replied with these words: "Thou art not true to the promise made when I left my father's house in Iceland." Biarne replied: "In this thing I do not see any other way;" continuing, "What course can you suggest?" He said, "I see this, that we change places and thou come up here and I go there." Biarne replied: "Let it be so, since I see that you are so anxious to live, and are frightened by the prospect of death." Then they changed places, and he descended into the boat with the men, and Biarne went up into the ship. And it is related that Biarne, and the sailors with him in the ship, perished in the worm sea. Those who went in the boat, went on their course until they came to land, where they told all these things.

After the next summer, Karlsefne went to Iceland with his son Snorre, and he went to his own home at Reikianess. The daughter of Snorre, son of Karlsefne, was Hallfrida, mother to Bishop Thorlak Runolfson. They had a son named Thorbiorn, whose daughter was named Thoruna, mother of Bishop Biarne. Thorgeir was the name of the other son of Snorre Karlsefne's son, father to Ingveld, and mother of the first bishop of Brand. And this is the end of the history.

THIRD NARRATIVE.

That same summer came a ship from Norway to Greenland. The man was called Thorfinn Karlsefne, who steered the ship. He was a son of Thord Hesthöfde, a son of Snorre Thordarson, from Höfda. Thorfinn Karlsefne was a man of great wealth, and was in Brattahlid with Leif Ericsson. Soon he fell in love with Gudrid, and courted her, and she referred to Leif to answer for her. Afterwards she was betrothed to him, and their wedding was held the same winter. At this time, as before, much was spoken about a Vinland voyage; and both Gudrid and others persuaded Karlsefne much to that expedition. Now this expedition was resolved upon, and they got ready a crew of sixty men, and five women;[1] and then they made the agreement, Karlsefne and his people, that each of them should have equal share in what they made of gain. They had with them all kinds of cattle,[2] having the intention to settle in the land, if they could. Karlsefne asked Leif for his houses in Vinland, but he said he would lend them, but not give them. Then they put to sea with the ship, and came to Leif's houses[3] safe, and carried up their goods, They soon had in hand a great and good prize, for a

---

[1] There were three ships in the expedition, and this was doubtless the company that went in one of them.

[2] These could be easily carried, especially as their cattle were small. All the early Portuguese expeditions carried their live stock with them. See *Prince Henry the Navigator.*

[3] The different events are here stated with some rapidity, and we seem to reach Leif's booths or huts sooner than necessary. According to the two previous accounts, they did not reach the locality of Leif's booths until the summer after they found the whale. These booths were at Mt. Hope Bay. This is either the result of confusion in the mind of the writer, or else it is founded on the fact that Leif erected habitations at *both* places. In the two first accounts of Thorfinn Karlsefne's expedition, they are not alluded to. There may be no real contradiction after all.

whale had been driven on shore, both large and excellent.[1] They went to it and cut it up, and had no want of food. Their cattle went up into the land; but soon they were unruly, and gave trouble to them. They had one bull with them. Karlsefne let wood be felled and hewed for shipping it, and had it laid on a rock to dry. They had all the good of the products of the land, which were these: both grapes and wood, and other products. After that first winter, and when summer came, [A. D. 1008.] they were aware of Skrællings being there; and a great troop of men came out of the woods. The cattle were near to them, and the bull began to bellow and roar very loud, and with that the Skrællings were frightened, and made off with their bundles — and these were of furs and sables and all sorts of skins; and they turned and wanted to go into the houses, but Karlsefne defended the doors. Neither party understood the language of the other. Then the Skrællings took their bundles and opened them, and wanted to have weapons in exchange for them, but Karlsefne forbade his men to sell weapons. Then he adopted this plan with them, that he told the women to bear out milk and dairy products to them; and when they saw these things, they would buy them and nothing else. And now the trade for the

---

[1] The other accounts say that the whale made them sick; but that was not because the flesh of the whale was spoiled. Beamish, in his translation of the song of Thorhall, indeed makes that disagreeable pagan tell his comrades, that, if they wish, they

"*Fetid* whales may boil
Here on Furdustrand
Far from Fatherland;"

but there is nothing in the text to throw suspicion upon the whale. The trouble was, that a sudden overfeeding caused nausea, and the whale was thrown away afterwards in religious disgust. Yet the event is out of its chronological order, and properly belongs in the account of the next year.

Skrællings was such, that they carried away their winnings in their stomachs; and Karlsefne and his comrades got both their bags and skin goods, and so they went away. And now it is to be told, that Karlsefne let a good strong fence be made around the habitation, and strengthened it for defense. At this time, Gudrid,[1] Karlsefne's wife, lay in of a male child, and the child was called Snorre. In the beginning of the next winter, came the Skrællings again to them, and in much greater numbers than before, and with the same kind of wares. Then said Karlsefne to the women, "Now ye shall carry out the same kind of food as was best liked the last time, and nothing else. And when they saw that they threw their bundles in over the fence: and Gudrid sat in the door within, by the cradle of Snorre, her son. Then came a shadow to the door, and a woman went in with a black kirtle on, rather short, with a snood around her head; clear, yellow hair; pale; with large eyes, so large that none ever saw such eyes in a human head. She went to where Gudrid was sitting, and said: "What art thou called?" "I am called Gudrid; and what art thou called?" "I am called Gudrid, said she." Then the goodwife, Gudrid, put out her hand to her, that she might sit down beside her. And at the same time Gudrid heard a great noise, and the woman had vanished;[2] and at the same time one of the Skrællings was killed by one of Karlsefne's house men, because he was about to take one of their weapons; and they made off as soon as possible, leaving behind them goods and clothes. No one had seen this woman but Gudrid. "Now," says Karlsefne, "we must be cautious, and take counsel; for I think they

---

[1] This event belongs to the previous year. These facts are not given in the other accounts, the writer appearing to have different information.

[2] This is another somewhat marvelous occurrence, similar to those with which Cotton Mather and others were accustomed to embellish New England history.

will come the third time with hostility and many people. We shall now take the plan, that ten men go out to the ness and show themselves there, and the rest of our men shall go into the woods and make a clearance for our cattle against the time the enemy comes out of the forest; and we shall take the bull before us, and let him go in front." And it happened so that at the place where they were to meet, there was a lake on the one side, and the forest on the other. The plan which Karlsefne had laid down, was adopted. The Skrællings came to the place where Karlsefne proposed to fight; and there was a battle there, and many of the Skrællings fell. There was one stout, handsome man among the Skrællings people, and Karlsefne thought that he must be their chief. One of the Skrællings had taken up an axe and looked at it awhile, and wielded it against one of his comrades and cut him down, so that he fell dead instantly. Then the stout man took the axe,[1] looked at it awhile, and threw it into the sea as far as he could. They then fled to the woods as fast as they could, and so ended the fight. Karlsefne stayed there with his men the whole winter; but towards spring he made known that he would not stay there any longer, and would return to Greenland.[2] Now they prepared for their voyage and took much goods from thence — vines, grapes and skin wares. They put to sea, and their ship came to Ericsfiord, and they there passed the winter.

---

[1] For the previous versions of this affair of the axe, see pp. 60. This last account appears a little plainer.

[2] It is true that he decided to leave the country, but he did not carry out his intention until the following year, 1010. This narrative skips over all the events of the third year. It is nevertheless given, in order that the reader may have the fullest possible knowledge of any shortcomings that may exist in the manuscripts. This is done with the more confidence, for the reason that there is no doubt but that all the narratives contain a broad substratum of solid truth.

The following summer,[1] [A. D. 1011.] Karlsefne went to Iceland and Gudrid with him, and he went home to Reikianess. His mother felt that he had made a poor match, and for this reason Gudrid was not at home the first winter. But when she saw that Gudrid was a noble woman, she went home, and they got on well together. Halfrid was the daughter of Snorre Karlsefnesson, mother to Bishop Thorlak Runolfson. Their son was named Thorbiorn, and his daughter, Thoruna, mother to Bishop Biorne. Thorgeir was the son of Snorre Karlsefnesson, father to Ingveld, mother of the first Bishop Brand. Snorre Karlsefnesson had a daughter, Steinun, who married Einar, son of Grundarketil, son of Thorvald Krok, the son of Thorer, of Espihol; their son was Thorstein Rauglatr. He was father to Gudrun, who married Jorund of Keldum. Halla was their daughter, and she was mother to Flose, father of Valgerda, who was mother of Herr Erland Sterka, father of Herr Hauk, the Lagman.[2] Another daughter of Flose was Thordis, mother of Fru Ingigerd the Rich; her daughter was Fru Hallbera, Abbess of Stad, in Reikianess. Many other distinguished men in Iceland are the descendants of Karlsefne and Thurid, who are not here mentioned. God be with us. Amen.

---

[1] From the statement at the end of the voyage of Freydis (see p. 80), we learn that the summer in which he returned from Iceland, Karlsefne went to Norway, and from thence the following spring, to Iceland. This does not conflict with the statement in the above narrative, though at first it may *appear* to. It does not say that he went the following summer from *Greenland* to Iceland, but that on that summer, he *went* to Iceland, which is perfectly true, though poorly stated, and his previous voyage to Norway being ignored.

[2] See p. 48.

VIII. THE VOYAGE OF FREYDIS, HELGE AND FINBOGE.

This narrative is found in *Antiquitates Americanæ*, p. 65. It shows that history, among the Icelanders, was not made subservient to family interests. At the conclusion we have a (supplementary) notice of Thorfinn and Gudrid, after their return to Iceland.

Now the conversation began again to turn upon a Vinland voyage, as the expedition was both gainful and honorable. The same summer [A. D. 1010.] that Karlsefne returned from Vinland, a ship arrived in Greenland from Norway. Two brothers commanded the ship, Helge and Finboge; and they remained that winter in Greenland. The brothers were of Icelandic descent from Earlfiord. It is now to be told, that Freydis, Eric's daughter, came home from Garda,[1] and went to the abode of Finboge and Helge, and proposed to them that they should go to Vinland with their vessel, and have half with her of all the goods they could get there. They agreed to this. Then she went to the abode of her brother Leif, and asked him to give her the houses he had built in Vinland; and he answered as before, that he would lend, but not give the houses. It was agreed upon between the brothers and Freydis, that each should have thirty fighting men, besides women. But Freydis broke this, and had five men more, and concealed them; and the brothers knew nothing of it until they arrived in Vinland.[2] They went to sea, and had

---

[1] Garda was the Episcopal seat of Greenland. Freydis and her husband went to Vinland with Karlsefne. It was she who frightened the Skrællings.

[2] It appears that the route to Vinland had become so well known, that the Saga writers no longer thought it necessary to describe it.

agreed beforehand to sail in company, if they could do so: and the difference was little, although the brothers came a little earlier, and had carried up their baggage to Leif's houses. And when Freydis came to the land, her people cleared the ship, and carried her baggage also up to the house. Then said Freydis: "Why are you carrying your things in here?" "Because we thought," said they, "that the whole of the agreement with us should be held." She said, "Leif lent the houses to me, not to you." Then said Helge, "In evil, we brothers cannot strive with thee:" and bore out their luggage and made a shed, and built it farther from the sea, on the borders of a lake,[1] and set all about it in order. Freydis let trees be cut down for her ship's cargo. Now winter set in, and the brothers proposed to have some games for amusement to pass the time. So it was done for a time, till discord came among them, and the games were given up, and none went from one house to the other; and things went on so during a great part of the winter. It happened one morning that Freydis got out of her berth, and put on her clothes, but not her shoes; and the weather was such that much dew had fallen. She took the cloak of her husband over her, and went out, and went to the house of the brothers, and to the door. A man had gone out a little before and left the door behind him, half shut. She opened the door, and stood in the doorway a little, and was silent. Finboge lay the farthest inside the hut, and was awake. He said: "What wilt thou have here, Freydis?" She said, "I want thee to get up and go out with me, for I would speak with thee."

---

[1] Mount Hope bay is still often called a lake. These waters always appear like lakes. Brereton, in his account of Gosnold's voyage, calls these same bays, lakes. He writes: "From this [Elizabeth] island, we went right over to the mayne, where we stood awhile as ravished at the beautie and dilicacy of the sweetnesse, besides divers cleare lakes, whereof we saw no end."

He did so: they went to a tree that was lying under the eaves of the hut, and sat down. "How dost thou like this place?" said she. He said, "The country, methinks, is good; but I do not like this quarrel that has arisen among us, for I think there is no cause for it." "Thou art right," says she, "and I think so too; and it is my errand to thy dwelling, that I want to buy the ship of your brothers, as your ship is larger than mine, and I would break up from hence." "I will let it be so," said he, "if that will please thee." Now they parted so, and she went home, and Finboge to his bed. She went up into her berth, and with her cold feet awakened Thorvard, who asked why she was so cold and wet. She answered with great warmth, "I went to these brothers," said she, "to treat about their ship, for I want a larger ship;[1] and they took it so ill, that they struck and abused me. And, thou, useless man! wilt neither avenge my affront, nor thy own; and now must I feel that I am away from Greenland, but I will separate[2] from thee if thou dost not avenge this." And now he could not bear her reproaches, and told his men to rise as fast as possible, and take their weapons. They did so, and went to the tents of the brothers, and went in as they lay asleep, and seized them all, bound them, and led them out bound, one after the other, and Freydis had each of them put to death, as he came out. Now all the men were killed; but the women were left, and nobody would kill them. Then said Freydis, "Give me an axe in my hand." This was done, and she turned on those five women, and did not give over until they were all dead. Now they returned to their own hut after this evil deed; and the people could only observe that Freydis thought

---

[1] Freydis was evidently the principal in all things.
[2] By the Icelandic law, a woman could separate from her husband for a slight cause.

she had done exceedingly well; and she said to her comrades, "If it be our lot to return to Greenland, I shall take the life of the man who speaks of this affair; and we shall say that we left them here when we went away." Now they got ready the ship early in spring [A. D. 1011.] which had belonged to the brothers, with all the goods they could get on, that the ship would carry, sailed out to sea, and had a good voyage; and the ship came early in the summer to Ericsfiord. Karlsefne was there still,[1] and had his ship ready for sea, but waited a wind; and it was a common saying that never a richer ship sailed from Greenland than that which he steered.

Freydis went home now to her house, which had stood without damage in the meanwhile. She bestowed many gifts on her followers, that they might conceal her wickedness; and she remained now on her farm. All were not so silent about their misdeeds and wickedness, that something did not come up about it. This came at last to the ears of Leif, her brother, and he thought this report was very bad. Leif took three men of Freydis's followers, and tortured them to speak, and they acknowledged the whole affair, and their tales agreed together. "I do not care," says Leif, "to treat my sister as she deserves; but this I will foretell them, that their posterity will never thrive." And it went so that nobody thought anything of them but evil, from that time.[2] Now we have to say that Karlsefne got ready his ship, and sailed out to sea.[3] He came on well, and reached Norway safely, and remained there all winter

---

[1] According to this statement, the expedition returned very early, as Karlsefne went to Norway the same season, as previously told.

[2] If this transaction had occurred during the previous century, when paganism universally prevailed, this atrocious act of the cold-blooded Freydis, would have been the prelude to almost endless strife.

[3] This account is supplementary to the foregoing, and is taken from the same work. Karlsefne, of course, sailed from Greenland.

and sold his wares; and he, and his wife, were held in esteem by the best people in Norway. Now in the following spring, he fitted out his ship for Iceland, and when he was quite ready, and his ship lay outside the pier waiting a wind, there came to him a south-country man, from Bremen, in Saxon land, who would deal with him for his house-bar.[1] "I will not sell it," said he. "I will give thee half a mark of gold for it," said the south-country man. Karlsefne thought it was a good offer, and sold it accordingly. The south-country man went away with his house-bar, and Karlsefne did not know what wood it was. It was massur-wood[2] from Vinland. Now Karlsefne put to sea, [A. D. 1012.] and his ship came to land north at Skagafiord,[3] and there he put up his vessel for winter. In spring he purchased Glambæirland,[4] where he took up his abode, and dwelt there as long as he lived, and was a man of great consideration; and many men are descended from him and his wife Gudrid, and it was a good family. When Karlsefne died, Gudrid took the management of his estates, and of Snorre her son, who was born in Vinland. And when Snorre was married, Gudrid went out of the country, and went to the south,[5] and came back again to

---

[1] *Húsasnotru* has been translated "house-besom." The exact meaning is not known. A besom-shaft would be too small, however rare the wood, to be made into anything of value. The bar for securing the house door was as common as necessary in every house, and this, perhaps, is what is referred to.

[2] See note 1, p. 36.

[3] In the north of Iceland.

[4] Not far from Skagafiord.

[5] It is understood that she went to Rome. It may be asked why she did not spread the news of her son's voyage in those parts of Europe whither she went, and make known the discovery of the New World. To this it may be replied, that the Icelanders had no idea that they had found a New World, and did not appreciate the value of their geographical knowledge. Besides, there is nothing to prove that Gudrid, and others who

Snorre's estate, and he had built a church at Glambæ. Afterwards Gudrid became a nun, and lived a hermit's life, and did so as long as she lived.[1] Snorre had a son called Thorgeir, who was father to Bishop Brand's mother, Ingveld. The daughter of Snorre Karlsefnesson was called Halfrid. She was mother of Runolf, the father of Bishop Thorlak. Karlsefne and Gudrid also had a son called Biörn. He was father of Thoruna, the mother of Bishop Biörn. Many people are descended from Karlsefne, and his kin have been lucky; and Karlsefne has given the most particular accounts of all these travels, of which something is here related.

---

went to Europe at this period, did *not* make known the Icelandic discoveries. At that time no interest was taken in such subjects, and therefore we have no right to expect to find traces of discussion in relation to what, among a very small class, would be regarded, at the best, as a curious story. See note on Adam of Bremen in the General Introduction.

[1] It will be remembered that all this was foretold by her former husband, Thorstein Ericson, when he returned to life in the house of Thorstein Black, in Greenland; from which we must infer that the voyage of Thorstein Ericson was composed after, or during, the second widowhood of Gudrid, and that the circumstance of Thorstein's prophecy, was, in accordance with the spirit of the age, imagined in order to meet the circumstances of the case. See p. 46.

MINOR NARRATIVES.

MINOR NARRATIVES.

I. ARE MARSON IN HVITRAMANNA-LAND.

This narrative is from the *Landnama-bok*, No. 107. Folio; collated with Hauksbok, Melabok and other manuscripts, in the *Arnæ-Magnæan* Collection.

It has frequently been observed that the *Landnama-bok* is of the highest authority; yet we must remember that it only proves the fact, that Rafn, the Limerick merchant, conveyed the narrative to Iceland from Ireland, where the circumstances were well known. The *Landnama-bok*, while it gives a tacit approval of the statements of the narrative, does not enter upon the question of the locality of the place to which Are Marson went. Therefore while we accept the narrative as genuine history, we should exercise due caution in determining the locality of Hvitramanna-land. Nothing is to be gained by making any forced deductions from the narrative; especially as the pre-Columbian discovery of America is abundantly proved, without the aid of this, or any other of the Minor Narratives.

Ulf the Squinter, son of Hogni the White, took the whole of Reikianess between Thorkafiord and Hafrafell; he married Biörg, daughter of Eyvind the Eastman,[1] sister

---

[1] That is, a Norwegian.

to Helge the Lean. They had a son named Atli the Red, who married Thorbiorg, sister of Steinolf the Humble. Their son was named Mar of Holum, who married Thorkatla, daughter of Hergil Neprass. She had a son named Are, who [A. D. 928.] was driven by a storm to Whiteman's land,[1] which some call Ireland the Great, which lies

---

[1] *Hvitramanna-land.* It will be remembered that in the Saga of Thorfinn Karlsefne (p. 63), this land was referred to by the natives whom he took prisoners. They described it as a land inhabited by a people who wore white clothes, carried poles before them, and shouted. Yet the Saga writer there says no more than that the people *think* that this was the place known as Ireland the Great. What the Skrællings say does not identify it with the land of Are Marson. Yet, in order to allow Professor Rafn, who held that this country was America, the full benefit of his theory, we give the following extract from Wafer's *Voyage*, which shows that in the year 1681, when he visited the Isthmus of Darien, there were people among the natives who answered tolerably well to the description given in Karlsefne's narrative. Wafer says: "They are white, and there are them of both sexes; yet there were few of them in comparison of the copper colored, possibly but one, to two or three hundred. They differ from the other Indians, chiefly in respect of color, though not in that only. Their skins are not of such a white, as those of fair people among Europeans, with some tincture of a blush or sanguine complexion; neither is their complexion like that of our paler people, but 'tis rather a Milkwhite, lighter than the color of any Europeans, and much like that of a white horse. . . . . Their bodies are beset all over, more or less, with a fine, short, milk-white down. . . . . The men would probably have white bristles for beards, did they not prevent them by their custom of plucking the young beard up by the roots. . . . . Their eyebrows are milk-white also, and so is the hair of their heads." p. 107.

He also adds, that "The men have a value for Cloaths, and if any of them had an old shirt given him by any of us, he would be sure to wear it, and strut about at no ordinary rate. Besides this, they have a sort of long cotton garments of their own, some white, and others of a rusty black, shaped like our carter's frocks, hanging down to their heels, with a fringe of the same of cotton, about a span long, and short, wide, open sleeves, reaching but to the middle of their arms. . . . They are worn on some great occasions. . . . When they are assembled, they will sometimes walk about the place or plantation where they are, with these, their robes on. And once I saw Tacenta thus walking with two or three hundred of

in the Western ocean opposite Vinland, six[1] days sail west of Ireland. Are was not allowed to go away, and was baptized[2] there. This was first told by Rafn, the Lime-

---

those attending him, as if he was mustering them. And I took notice that those in the black gowns walked before him, and the white after him, each having their lances of the same color with their robes." But notwithstanding these resemblances, historians will ask for more solid proof of the identity of the two people.

[1] Professor Rafn in, what seems to the author, his needless anxiety to fix the locality of the 'White-man's land in America, says that, as this part of the manuscript is difficult to decipher, the original letters *may* have got changed, and vi inserted instead of xx, or xi, which numerals would afford time for the voyager to reach the coast of America, in the vicinity of Florida. Smith in his *Dialogues*, has even gone so far as to *suppress* the term *six* altogether, and substitutes, " by a number of days sail unknown." This is simply trifling with the subject. In *Grönland's Historiske Mindesmærker*, chiefly the work of Finn Magnussen, no question is raised on this point. The various versions all give the number six, which limits the voyage to the vicinity of the Azores. Schöning, to whom we are so largely indebted for the best edition of Heimskringla, lays the scene of Marson's adventure at those islands, and suggests that they may at that time have covered a larger extent of territory than the present, and that they may have suffered from earthquakes and floods, adding, " It is likely, and all circumstances show, that the said land has been a piece of North America." This is a bold, though not very unreasonable hypothesis, especially as the volcanic character of the islands is well known. In 1808, a volcano rose to the height of 3,500 feet. Yet Schöning's suggestion is not needed. The fact that the islands were not inhabited when discovered by the Portuguese does not, however, settle anything against Schöning, because in the course of five hundred years, the people might either have migrated, or been swept away by pestilence. *Grönland's Historiske Mindesmærker*, (vol. I, p. 150), says simply, that " It is *thought* that he (Are Marson) ended his days in America, or at all events in one of the larger islands of the west. Some think that it was one of the Azore islands."

[2] The fact that Are Marson is said to have been baptized in Ireland the Great, does not prove that the place, wherever located, was inhabited by a colony of Irish Christians. Yet this view was urged by Professor Rafn and others, who held that Great Ireland was situated in Florida. A Shawanese *tradition* is given to prove that Florida was early settled by white men from over the sea. We read that in 1818, " the Shawanese were established in Ohio, whither they came from Florida, Black Hoof, then

rick trader, who lived for a long time in Ireland. So also Thorkel, son of Geller, tells that certain Icelanders said, who heard Thorfinn, Earl of the Orkneys, say, that Are had been seen and known in White-man's land, and that, though not allowed to leave, he was held in much honor. Are had a wife named Thorgeir, daughter of Alf of Dolum. Their sons were Thorgils, Gudleif and Illuge, which is the family of Reikianess. Jorund was the son of Ulf the Squinter. He married Thorbiorg Knarrabringa. They had a daughter, Thorhild, whom Eric the Red married. They had a son, Leif the Fortunate of Greenland. Jorund was the name of the son of Atli the Red; he married Thordis, daughter of Thorgeir Suda; their daughter was Thorkatla, who married Thorgils Kollson. Jorund was also the father of Snorre.[1]

---

eighty-five years old, was born there, and remembered bathing in the sea. He told the Indian Agent, that the people of his tribe had a tradition, that their ancestors came over the sea, and that for a long time they kept a yearly sacrifice for their safe arrival."—*Archæologia Americana*, vol. I, p. 273. Yet these Indians, the supposed descendants of eminently pious Christians from Ireland, were bitterly opposed to Christianity, and had no Christian traditions. This view requires altogether too much credulity. Is it not more reasonable, especially in view of the fact that this narrative is not needed in demonstrating the pre-Columbian discovery of America — to seek for the White-man's land in some island of the Atlantic; for if we were to allow that six, should mean eleven or twenty days sail, we should not be much better off, since there is so much difficulty in finding the white men for the land in question.

[1] It will appear from this genealogical account, that Are Marson was no obscure or mythological character. In 981 he was one of the principal men of Iceland, and is highly spoken of. Yet his connection with Ireland the Great, though undoubtedly real, hardly *proves*, what may nevertheless be true — a pre-Scandinavian discovery of America by the Irish. This, not improbable view, demands clearer proof, and will repay investigation. The other characters mentioned are equally well known. See *Antiquitates Americanæ*, pp. 211–12.

II. BIÖRN ASBRANDSON.

This narrative is taken from Eyrbyggia Saga, which contains the early history of that part of Iceland lying around Snæfells, on the west coast. The Saga is not of a later date than the thirteenth century. It is given here, not because it applies largely to the question under consideration, the pre-Columbian discovery of America, but rather because it will make the reader fully acquainted with the hero, who afterwards appears.

Bork the Fat, and Thordis, daughter of Sur, had a daughter named Thurid, who married Thorbiörn the Fat, living on the estate of Froda. He was a son of Orne the Lean, who held and tilled the farm of Froda. Thorbiörn had before been married to Thurid, daughter of Asbrand, of Kamb, in Breidavik, and sister of Biörn Breidaviking the Athlete, soon to be mentioned in this Saga, and of Arnbiörn the Handy. The sons of Thorbiörn and Thurid, were Ketil the Champion, Gunnlaug and Hallstein.

Now this must be related of Snorre the Priest,[1] that he undertook the suit for the slaying of Thorbiörn, his kinsman. He also caused his sister to remove to his own home, at Helgefell, because it was reported that Biörn Asbrand, of Kamb, had come to pay her improper attention.

---

[1] Priest or *Gode*. This was the heathen priest of Iceland, whose duty was to provide the temple offerings, for which purpose a contribution was made by every farm in the vicinity. This office was also united with that of chief, judge, and advocate, and for the cases conducted by him at the Thing, he received the customary fees; yet he was obliged to depend for his support, mainly upon the products of his farm. The office was hereditary, but could be sold, assigned, or forfeited.

There was a man named Thorodd, of Medalfells Strand, an upright man and a good merchant. He owned a trading vessel in which he sailed to distant lands. Thorodd had sailed to the west,[1] to Dublin, on a trading voyage. At that time, Sigurd [2] Hlodverson, Earl of the Orkneys, had made an expedition towards the west, to the Hebrides and the Man, and had laid a tribute upon the habitable part of Man. Having settled the peace, he left men to collect the tribute; the earl himself returned to the Orkneys. Those who were left to collect the tribute, got all ready and set sail with a southwest wind. But after they had sailed some time, to the southeast and east, a great storm arose, which drove them to the northward as far as Ireland, and their vessel was cast away on a barren, uninhabited island. Just as they reached the island, Thorodd the Icelander came sailing by from Dublin. The shipwrecked men begged for aid. Thorodd put out a boat and went to them himself. When he reached them, the agents of Sigurd promised him money if he would carry them to their home in the Orkneys. When he told them that he could by no means do so, as he had made all ready to go back to Iceland, they begged the harder, believing that neither their money nor their liberty would be safe in Ireland or the Hebrides, whither they had just before been with a hostile army. At length Thorodd came to this, that he would sell them his ship's long-boat for a large sum of the tribute money; in this they reached the Orkneys, and Thorodd sailed to Iceland without a boat. Having reached the southern shores of the island, he laid his course along the coast to the westward, and entered Breidafiord, and came to the harbor

---

[1] It was west with regard to Norway, the people being accustomed to use this expression.

[2] Killed in Ireland in a battle, 1013.

at Dögurdarness. The same autumn he went to Helgefell to spend the winter with Snorre the Priest; and from that time he was called Thorodd the Tribute Taker. This took place just after the murder of Thorbiörn the Fat. During the same winter, Thurid, the sister of Snorre the Priest, who had been the wife of Thorbiörn the Fat, was at Helgefell. Thorodd made proposals of marriage to Snorre the Priest, with respect to Thurid. Being rich, and known by Snorre to be of good repute, and that he would be useful in supporting his administration of affairs, he consented. Therefore their marriage was celebrated during this winter, at Snorre's house, at Helgefell. In the following spring, Thorodd set himself up at Froda, and was thought an upright man. But when Thurid went to Froda, Biörn Asbrandson often paid her visits, and it was commonly reported that he had corrupted her chastity. Thorodd vainly tried to put an end to these visits. At that time Thorodd Wooden Clog lived at Arnahval. His sons, Ord and Val were men grown and youths of the greatest promise. The men blamed Thorodd for allowing himself to be insulted so greatly by Biörn, and offered him their aid, if desired, to end his coming. It chanced one time when Biörn came to Froda, that he sat with Thurid talking. It was Thorodd's custom when Biörn was there to sit in the house. But he was now nowhere to be seen. Then Thurid said, " Take care, Biörn, for I fear Thorodd means to put a stop to your visits here; I think he has secured the road, and means to attack you, and overpower you with unequal numbers." Biörn replied, " That is possible," and then sang these verses:

> O Goddess[1] whom bracelet adorns,
> This day (I linger

---

[1] Literally, *woman*, with reference to Jörd, the Earth, one of the wives of Odin, and also mother of Thor.

>In my beloved's arms)
>Stay longest in the heavens,
>As we both must wish;
>For I this night am drawn
>To drink myself the parentals [1]
>Of my oft-departing joys.

Having done this, Biörn took his weapons, and went to return home. As he went up the hill Digramula, five men jumped out upon him from their hiding place. These were Thorodd and two of his men, and the sons of Thoror Wooden Clog. They attacked Biörn, but he defended himself bravely and well. The sons of Thoror pressed him sharply, but he slew them both. Thorodd then fled with his men, though he himself had only a slight wound, and the others not any. Biörn went on until he reached home, and entered the house. The lady of the house [2] ordered a maid to place food before him. When the maid came into the room with the light, and saw Biörn wounded, she went and told Asbrand his father, that Biörn had returned, covered with blood. Asbrand came into the room, and inquired what was the cause of his wounds. He said, "Have you and Thorodd had a fight!" Biörn replied that it was so. Asbrand asked how the affair ended. Böirn replied with these verses:

>Not so easy against a brave man
>It is to fight;
>(Wooden Clog's two sons
>Now I have slain).
>As for the ship's commander,
>A woman to embrace,
>Or for the cowardly,
>A golden tribute to buy. [3]

---

[1] Funeral cups.
[2] Biörn's mother.
[3] This is a fling at Thorodd the Tribute Taker.

Asbrand bound up his son's wounds, and his strength was soon restored. Thorodd went to Snorre the Priest, to talk with him about setting a suit on foot against Biörn, on account of the killing of Thoror's sons. This suit was laid in the court of Thorsnesthing. It was settled that Asbrand, who became surety for his son, should pay the usual fines. Biörn was exiled for three years,[1] and went abroad the same summer. During that summer, a son was born to Thurid, who was called Kiarten. He grew up at home, in Froda, and early gave great hope and promise.

When Biörn crossed the sea he came into Denmark, and went thence to Jomsberg. At that time, Palnatoki was captain of the Jomsberg[2] Vikings. Biörn was admitted into the crew, and won the name of the Athlete. He was at Jomsberg when Styrbiörn the Hardy, assaulted it. He went into Sweden, when the Jomsberg Vikings

---

[1] This shows, that while Biörn killed the men in self defense, it was the opinion of the court that he did not get what he deserved.

[2] Jomsberg was the head quarters of an order of vikings or pirates, where a castle was also built by King Harold Blaatand, of Denmark. It was situated on one of the outlets of the Oder, on the coast of Pomerania. It was probably identical with Julian, founded by the Wends, and was recognized as the island of Wallin, which Adam of Bremen, in the eleventh century, described as the largest and most flourishing commercial city in Europe. Burislaus, king of the Wends, surrendered the neighboring territory into the hands of Palnatoki, a great chief of Fionia, who was pledged to his support. Accordingly he built a stronghold here, and organized a band of pirates, *commonly* called vikings, though it must be observed, that while every viking was a pirate, every pirate was not a viking. Only those pirates of princely blood, were properly called vikings, or sea-kings. The Jomsvikings were distinguished for their rare courage, and for the fearlessness with which they faced death. They were governed by strict laws, and hedged about by exact requirements, and were also, it is said, pledged to celibacy. Jomsberg was destroyed about the year 1175, by Waldemar the Great, of Denmark, aided by the princes of Germany and the king of Barbarrossa. Those of the pirates who survived, escaped to a place near the mouth of the Elbe, where a few years after, they were

aided Styrbiörn;[1] he was in the battle of Tynsvall, in which Styrbiörn was killed, and escaped with the other Joms-vikings in the woods. While Palnatoki lived, Biörn remained with him, distinguished among all, as a man of remarkable courage.

The same summer [A. D. 996.] the brothers, Biörn and Arnbiörn returned into Iceland to Rönhavnsos. Biörn was always afterwards called the Athlete of Breidavik. Arnbiorn, who had gotten much wealth abroad, bought the Bakka estate in Raunhavn, the same summer. He lived there with little show or ostentation, and in most affairs was silent, but was, nevertheless, a man active in all things. Biörn, his brother, after his return from abroad, lived in splendor and elegance, for during his absence, he had truly adopted the manners of courtiers. He much excelled Arnbiörn in personal appearance, and was none the less active in execution. He was far more expert than his brother in martial exercises, having improved much abroad. The same summer after his return, there was a general meeting near Headbrink,[2] within the bay of Froda. All the merchants rode thither, clothed in colored garments, and there was a great assembly. Housewife

---

annihilated by the Danes, who in the reign of Canute VI, completely destroyed their stronghold. Accounts of their achievements may be found in the Saga of King Olaf Tryggvesson, in vol. I, of Laing's *Heimskringla*. The Icelanders sometimes joined the Norway pirates, as was the case with Biörn, but they did not fit out pirate ships. Palnatoki died in the year 993.

[1] Styrbiörn, son of King Olaf, ruled Sweden in connection with Eric, called the Victorious. Styrbiörn's ambition, to which was added the crime of murder, led to his disgrace. He joined the vikings, adding sixty ships to their force. He was killed, as stated, in 984, in a battle with his uncle near Upsula.

[2] Dasent says in describing the coast: "Now we near the stupendous crags of Hofdabrekka, Headbrink, where the mountains almost stride into the main."

Thurid, of Froda, was there, with whom Biörn began to talk; no one censuring, because they expected their conversation would be long, as they had not seen each other for a great while. On the same day there was a fight, and one of the Nordenfield men was mortally wounded, and was carried down under a bush on the beach; so much blood flowed out of the wound, that there was a large pool of blood in the bush. The boy Kiarten, Thurid of Fróda's son, was there; he had a little axe in his hand, and ran to the bush and dipped the axe in the blood. When the Sondensfield's men rode from the beach south, Thord Blig asked Biörn how the conversation between him and Thurid of Froda, ended. Biörn said that he was well satisfied. Then Thord asked if he had seen the boy Kiarten, their and Thorodd's son. "I saw him," said Biörn: "What is your opinion of him?" asked Thord. Biörn answered with the following song:

> " I saw a boy run
> With fearful eyes,
> The woman's image, to
> The wolf's well [1] in the wood;
> People will say,
> That his true father [was]
> He that ploughed the sea,
> This the boy does not know."

Thord said: " What will Thorodd say when he hears that the boy belongs to you?" Then Biörn sung:

> " Then will the noble born woman [make]
> Thorodd's suspicion
> Come true, when she gives me
> The same kind of sons;

---

[1] Referring to the dead man's blood.

> Always the slender,
> Snow-white woman loved me,
> I still to her
> Am a lover."

Thord said, it will be best for you not to have anything to do with each other, and that you turn your thoughts. "It is certainly a good idea," said Biörn, "but it is far from my intention; though there is some difference when I have to do with such men as her brother Snorre." "You must take care of your own business," said Thord, and that ended their talk. Biörn afterwards went home to Kamb, and took the affairs of the family into his own hands, for his father was now dead. The following winter he determined to make a journey over the hills, to Thurid. Although Thorodd disliked this, he nevertheless saw that it was not easy to prevent its occurrence, since before he was defeated by him, and Biörn was much stronger, and more skilled in arms than before. Therefore he bribed Thorgrim Galdrakin to raise a snow storm against Biörn when he crossed the hills. When a day came, Biörn made a journey to Froda. When he proposed to return home, the sky was dark and the snow storm began. When he ascended the hills, the cold became intense, and the snow fell so thickly that he could not see his way. Soon the strength of the storm increased so much that he could hardly walk. His clothes, already wet through, froze around his body, and he wandered, he did not know where. In the course of the night he reached a cave, and in this cold house he passed the night. Then Biörn sung:

> "Woman that bringest
> Vestments,[1] would
> Not like my
> Dwelling in such a storm

---

[1] In Iceland the women are accustomed to bring travelers dry clothes.

> If she knew that
> He who before steered ships,
> Now in the rock cave
> Lay stiff and cold."

Again he sang:

> " The cold field of the swans,
> From the east with loaded ship I ploughed,
> Because the woman inspired me with love;
> I know that I have great trouble suffered,
> And now, for a time, the hero is,
> Not in a woman's bed, but in a cave."

Biörn stayed three days in the cave, before the storm subsided; and on the fourth day he came home from the mountain to Kamb. He was very weary. The domestic asked him where he was during the storm. Biörn sung:

> " My deeds under
> Styrbiörn's proud banner are known.
> It came about that steel-clad Eric
> Slew men in battle;
> Now I on the wide heath,
> Lost my way [and],
> Could not in the witch-strong
> Storm, find the road." [1]

Biörn passed the rest of the winter at home; the following spring his brother Arnbiörn fixed his abode in Bakka, in Raunhafn, but Biörn lived at Kamb, and had a grand house.....

This same summer, Thorodd the Tribute Taker invited Snorre the Priest, his kinsman, to a feast at his house in Froda. Snorre went there with twenty men. In the

---

[1] All of these verses are extremely obscure and elliptical, though far more intelligible to the modern mind than the compositions which belonged to a still older period. All the chief men of Iceland practiced the composition of

course of the feast, Thorodd told Snorre how much he was hurt and disgraced by the visits of Biörn Asbrandson, to Thurid, his wife, Snorre's sister, saying that it was right for Snorre to do away with this scandal. Snorre after passing some days feasting with Thorodd went home with many presents. Then Snorre the Priest rode over the hills and spread the report that he was going down to his ship in the bay of Raunhafn. This happened in summer, in the time of haymaking. When he had gone as far south as the Kambian hills, Snorre said: "Now let us ride back from the hills to Kamb; let it be known to you," he added, "what I wish to do. I have resolved to attack and destroy Biörn. But I am not willing to attack and destroy him in his house, for it is a strong one, and Biörn is stout and active, while our number is small. Even those who with greater numbers, have attacked brave men in their houses, have fared badly; an example of which you know in the case of Gissur the White; who, when with eighty men, they attacked Gunnar[1] of Lithend, alone in his house, many were wounded and many were killed, and they would have been compelled to give up the attack, if Geir the Priest had not learned that Gunnar was short of arrows. Therefore," said he, "as we may expect to find Biörn out of doors, it being the time of haymaking, I appoint you my kinsman, Mar, to give him the first wound; but I would have you know this, that there is no room for child's play, and you must expect a contest with a hungry wolf, unless your first wound shall be his death blow." As they rode from the hills towards his homestead, they saw Biörn in the fields; he was making a sledge,[2]

---

verse. Chaucer makes his Parson apologize for his inability to imitate the practice.

[1] See the Saga of Burnt Nial.

[2] These sledges were used in drawing hay, as the roads were then, as now, too poor for carts.

and no one was near him. He had no weapon but a small axe, and a large knife in his hand of a span's length, which he used to round the holes in the sledge. Biörn saw Snorre riding down from the hills, and recognized them. Snorre the Priest had on a blue cloak, and rode first. The idea suddenly occurred to Biörn, that he ought to take his knife and go as fast as he could to meet them, and as soon as he reached them, lay hold of the sleeve of Snorre with one hand, and hold the knife in the other, so that he might be able to pierce Snorre to the heart, if he saw that his own safety required it. Going to meet them, Biörn gave them hail, and Snorre returned the salute. The hands of Mar fell, for he saw that if he attacked Biörn, the latter would at once kill Snorre. Then Biörn walked along with Snorre and his comrades, asked what was the news, keeping his hands as at first. Then he said: "I will not try to conceal, neighbor Snorre, that my present attitude and look seem threatening to you, which might appear wrong, but for that I have understood that your coming is hostile. Now I desire that if you have any business to transact with me, you will take another course than the one you intended, and that you will transact it openly. If none, I will that you make peace, which when done, I will return to my work, as I do not wish to be led about like a fool." Snorre replied: " Our meeting has so turned out that we shall at this time part in the same peace as before; but I desire to get a pledge from you, that from this time you will leave off visiting Thurid, because if you go on in this, there can never be any real friendship between us." Biörn replied: "This I will promise, and will keep it; but I do not know how I shall be able to keep it, so long as Thurid and I live in the same land." "There is nothing so great binding you here," said Snorre, "as to keep you from going to some other land." "What you now say is true," replied Biörn, "and so let it be, and let our meeting end with this pledge, that neither you nor Thorodd shall have any trouble from my visits to Thurid, in the next year." With this they parted. Snorre the Priest rode down to his ship, and then went home to Helgefell. The day after, Biörn rode south to Raunhafn, and engaged his passage in a ship for the same summer. [A. D. 999.] When all was ready they set sail with a northeast wind which blew during the greater part of that summer. Nothing was heard of the fate of the ship for a very long time.[1]

III. GUDLEIF GUDLAUGSON.

This narrative, which shows what became of Biörn Asbrandson, whose adventures are partially related in the previous sketch, is from the Eyrbyggia Saga. Notwithstanding the somewhat romantic character of these two narratives, there can be no doubt but that they are true histories. Yet that they relate to events in America, is not altogether so certain.

There was a man named Gudleif, the son of Gudlaug the Rich, of Straumfiord and brother of Thorfinn, from whom the Sturlingers are descended. Gudleif was a great merchant. He had a trading vessel, and Thorolf Eyrar Loptson had another, when they fought with Gyrid, son of Sigvald Earl. Gyrid lost an eye in that fight. It took place near the end of the reign of King Olaf the Saint, that Gudleif went on a trading voyage to the west to Dublin.

---

[1] This is the only paragraph which applies directly to the subject in hand. The following narrative will bring Biörn to notice again.

On his return to Iceland, sailing from the west of Ireland, he met with northeast winds, and was driven far into the ocean west, and southwest, so that no land was seen, the summer being now nearly gone. Many prayers were offered that they might escape from the sea. At length they saw land. It was of great extent, but they did not know what land it was. They took counsel and resolved to make for the land, thinking it unwise to contend with the violence of the sea. They found a good harbor, and soon after they went ashore, a number of men came down to them. They did not recognize the people, but thought that their language resembled the Irish.[1] In a short time such a number of men had gathered around them as numbered many hundred. These attacked them and bound them all and drove them inland. Afterwards they were brought before an assembly, and it was considered what should be done with them. They thought that some wished to kill and that others were for dividing them among the villages as slaves. While this was going on, they saw a great number of men riding[2] towards them with a banner conspicuously lifted up, whence they inferred that some great man was among them. And when the company drew near, they saw a man riding under the banner, tall and with a martial air, aged and grayhaired. All present treated this man with the utmost honor and deference. They soon saw that their case was referred to the decision of this man. He commanded Gudleif and his comrades to be brought before him, and coming into his presence he addressed them in the Northern tongue, and asked from

---

[1] Few persons will infer much from this; nothing is easier than to find resemblances in language.

[2] The language indicates that they were riding horseback, though it is not conclusive. And at the period referred to, there were no horses in America, they having been introduced by the Spaniards, after the discovery by Columbus. At least, such is the common opinion.

what land they came. They replied that the chief part were Icelanders. The man asked which of them were Icelanders. Gudleif declared himself to be an Icelander, and saluted the old man, which he received kindly, and asked what part of Iceland he came from. He replied that he came from the district some called Bogafiord. He asked who lived in Bogafiord, to which Gudleif replied at some length. Afterwards this man inquired particularly about all the principal men of Bogafiord and Breidafiord; and of these he inquired with special interest into everything relating to Snorre the Priest, and of his sister Thurid, of Froda, and for the great Kiarten, her son. In the meanwhile the natives grew impatient about the disposition of the sailors. Afterwards the great man left him and took twelve of the natives apart, and conferred with them. Afterwards he returned. Then the old man spoke to Gudleif and his comrades, and said: "We have had some debate concerning you, and the people have left the matter to my decision; I now permit you to go where you will, and although summer is nearly gone, I advise you to leave at once; for these people are of bad faith, and hard to deal with, and now think they have been deprived of their right." Then Gudleif asked, "Who shall we say, if we reach our own country again, to have given us our liberty?" He replied: "That, I will not tell you, for I am not willing that any of my friends or kindred should come here, and meet with such a fate as you would have met, but for me. Age now comes on so fast, that I may almost expect any hour to be my last. Though I may live some time longer, there are other men of greater influence than myself, though now at some distance from this place, and these would not grant safety or peace to any strange men." Then he looked to the fitting out of their ship, and stayed at this place until a fair wind sprang up, so that they might leave the port. Before they went away, this man took a gold ring from his hand and gave it to Gudleif, and also a good sword. Then he said to Gudleif: "If fortune permits you to reach Iceland, give this sword to Kiarten, hero of Froda, and this ring to Thurid, his mother." Gudleif asked, "Who shall I say was the sender of this valuable gift?" He replied: "Say that he sent it who loved the lady of Froda, better than her brother, the Priest of Helgafell. And if any man desires to know who sent this valuable gift, repeat my words, that I forbid any one to seek me, for it is a dangerous voyage, unless others should meet with the same fortune as you. This region is large, but has few good ports, and danger threatens strangers on all sides from the people, unless it shall fall to others as yourselves." After this they separated. Gudleif, with his comrades, went to sea, and reached Ireland the same autumn, and passed the winter in Dublin. The next spring they sailed to Iceland, and Gudleif delivered the jewel into the hand of Thurid. It was commonly believed that there was no doubt but that the man seen, was Biörn Breidaviking Kappa. And there is no other reliable report to prove this.

IV. ALLUSIONS TO VOYAGES FOUND IN ANCIENT MANUSCRIPTS.

Professor Rafn, in *Antiquitates Americanæ*, gives brief notices of numerous Icelandic voyages to America, and other lands at the west, of which there is now no record. The works in which they are found are of the highest respectability. It is only necessary here to give the facts, which have been collected with much care. They show that the pre-Columbian discovery of America has tinged nearly the whole body of Icelandic history, in which the subject is referred to, not as a matter of doubt, but as something perfectly well known. All these revelations combine to furnish indisputable proof of the positions maintained in this work, showing as they do, beyond all reasonable question, that the impression which so generally prevailed in regard to the discovery of this land, was not the result of a literary fraud. Some of the facts are given below:

1121. Eric, Bishop of Greenland,[1] went to search out Vinland.
Bishop Eric Upse sought Vinland.
1285. A new land is discovered west from Iceland.
New land is found......[2]
Adalbrand and Thorvald, the sons of Helge, found the new land.
Adalbrand and Thorvald found new land west of Iceland.
The Feather [3] Islands are discovered.
1288. Rolf is sent by King Eric to search out the new land, and called on people of Iceland to go with him.
1289. King Eric sends Rolf to Iceland to seek out the new land.
1290. Rolf traveled through Iceland, and called out men for a voyage to the new land.[1]

---

[1] This is found in *Annales Islandorum Regii*, which gives the history of Iceland from the beginning down to 1307. Also in *Annales Flateyensis*, and in *Annales Reseniini*. Eric was appointed bishop of Greenland, but performed no duties after his consecration, and eventually resigned that see, in order to undertake the mission to Vinland. He is also spoken of in two works, as going to Vinland with the title of Bishop of Greenland, a title which he had several years before his actual consecration.

[2] The manuscript is deficient here.

[3] The Feather Islands are mentioned in the *Lögmanns Annall*, or, Annals of the Governors of Iceland, and *Annales Skalholtini*, or Annals of the Bishopric of Skalholt, written in the middle of the fourteenth century, long before Columbus went to Iceland. Beamish suggests that these are the Penguin and Bacaloa Islands.

[4] "The notices of Nyja land and Duneyjar, would seem to refer to a re-discovery of some parts of the eastern coast of America, which had been

1295. Landa-Rolf died.
1357. There came thirteen large ships to Iceland. Eindride-suden was wrecked in East Borgafiord, near Langeness. The crew and the greater part of the cargo was saved. Bessalangen was wrecked outside of Sida. Of its crew, Haldor Magre and Gunthorm Stale, and nineteen men altogether, were drowned. The cargo suffered also. There were also six ships driven back. There came likewise a ship from Greenland,[1] smaller than the smallest of Iceland ships, that came in the outer bay. It had lost its anchor. There were seventeen men on board, who had gone to Markland,[2] and on their return were drifted here. But here altogether that winter, were eighteen large ships, besides the two that were wrecked in the summer.

There came a ship from Greenland that had sailed to Markland, and there were eight men on board.

V. GEOGRAPHICAL FRAGMENTS.

The first of these documents is from a work which professes to give a description of the earth in the middle age. From this it appears that the Icelanders had a correct idea of the location of Vinland in New England, though they did not comprehend the fact that they had discovered a

---

previously visited by earlier voyagers. The original appellation of Nyja land, or *Nyjafundu-land*, would have naturally led to the modern English name of Newfoundland, given by Cabot, to whose knowledge the discovery would [might ?] have come through the medium of the commercial intercourse between England and Iceland in the fifteenth century."—*Beamish.*

[1] See the Decline of Greenland, in Introduction.

[2] Markland (Woodland) was Nova Scotia, as we know from the description of Leif and others. These vessels doubtless went to get timber. All these accounts show that the Western ocean was generally navigated in the middle of the fourteenth century.

new Continent. The document may be found in *Antiquitates Americanæ*, p. 283. In the appendix of that work may be seen a *fac simile* of the original manuscript. The second document is from (*Antiquitates Americanæ*, p. 292). It was found originally in the miscellaneous collection called the *Gripla*.

A BRIEF DESCRIPTION OF THE WHOLE EARTH.

The earth is said to be divided into three parts. One of these is called Asia, and extends from northeast to southwest, and occupies the middle of the earth. In the eastern part are three separate regions, called Indialand. In the farthest India, the Apostle Bartholomew preached the faith; and where he likewise gave up his life (for the name of Christ). In the nearest India, the Apostle Thomas preached, and there also he suffered death for the cause of God. In that part of the earth called Asia, is the city of Nineveh, greatest of all cities. It is three days' journey in length and one day's journey in breadth. There is also the city of Babylon, ancient and very large. There King Nebuchadnezzar formerly reigned, but now that city is so thoroughly destroyed that it is not inhabited by men, on account of serpents and all manner of noxious creatures. In Asia is Jerusalem, and also Antioch; in this city Peter the Apostle founded an Episcopal seat, and where he, the first of all men, sang Mass. Asia Minor is a region of Great Asia. There the Apostle John preached, and there also, in the city Ephesus, is his tomb. They say that four rivers flow out of Paradise. One is called Pison or Ganges; this empties into the sea surrounding the world. Pison rises under a mountain called Orcobares. The second river flowing from Paradise, is called Tigris, and the third, Euphrates. Both empty into the Mediterranean (sea), near

Antioch. The Nile, also called Geon, is the fourth river that runs from Paradise. It separates Asia from Africa, and flows through the whole of Egypt. In Egypt is New Babylon (Cairo), and the city called Alexandria. The second part of the earth is called Africa, which extends from the southwest to the northwest. There are Serkland, and three regions called Blaland (land of blackmen or negroes). The Mediterranean sea divides Europe from Africa. Europe is the third part of the earth, extended from west and northwest to the northeast. In the east of Europe is the kingdom of Russia. There are Holmgard, Palteskia and Smalenskia. South of Russia lies the kingdom of Greece. Of this kingdom, the chief city is Constantinople, which our people call Miklagard. In Miklagard is a church, which the people call St. Sophia, but the Northmen call it Ægisif. This church exceeds all the other churches in the world, both as respects its structure and size. Bulgaria and a great many islands, called the Greek islands, belong to the kingdom of Greece. Crete and Cyprus are the most noted of the Greek islands. Sicily is a great kingdom in that part of the earth called Europe. Italy is a country south of the great ridge of mountains, called by us Mundia [Alps]. In the remotest part of Italy is Apulia, called by the Northmen, Pulsland. In the middle of Italy is Rome. In the north of Italy is Lombardy, which we call Lombardland. North of the mountains on the east, is Germany, and on the southwest is France. Hispania, which we call Spainland, is a great kingdom that extends south to the Mediterranean, between Lombardy and France. The Rhine is a great river that runs north from Mundia, between Germany and France. Near the outlets of the Rhine is Friesland, northward from the sea. North of Germany is Denmark. The ocean runs into the Baltic sea, near Denmark. Sweden lies east of Denmark, and Norway at the north. North of Norway is Finnmark.

The coast bends thence to the northeast, and then towards the east, until it reaches Permia, which is tributary to Russia. From Permia, desert tracts extend to the north, reaching as far as Greenland. Beyond Greenland, southward, is Helluland; beyond that is Markland; from thence it is not far to Vinland, which some men are of the opinion, extends to Africa.[1] England and Scotland are one island; but each is a separate kingdom. Ireland is a great island. Iceland is also a great island north of Ireland. All these countries are situated in that part of the world called Europe. Next to Denmark is Lesser Sweden; then is Oeland, then Gottland, then Helsingeland, then Vermeland, and the two Kvendlands, which lie north of Biarmeland. From Biarmeland stretches desert land towards the north, until Greenland begins. South of Greenland is Helluland; next is Markland, from thence it is not far to Vinland the Good, which some think goes out to Africa; and if this is so, the sea must extend between Vinland and Markland. It is told that Thorfinn Karlsefne cut wood here to ornament his house,[2] went afterwards to seek out Vinland the Good, and came there where they thought the land was, but did not reach it, and got none of the wealth of the land.[3] Leif the Lucky first discovered Vinland, and then he met some merchants in distress at sea, and by God's grace, saved their lives; and he introduced Christianity into Greenland, and it flourished so there that an Episcopal seat was set up in the place, called

---

[1] In the face of this and a multitude of similar statements, Mr. Bancroft endeavors to make his readers believe that the locality of Vinland was uncertain. He might, with equal propriety, tell us that the location of Massachusetts itself was uncertain, because, according to the original grant, it extended to the Pacific ocean.

[2] See note 1, p. 81.

[3] This is a blunder. The writer must have been more of a geographer than historian. See the Saga of Leif, p. 36.

Gardar. England and Scotland are an island, and yet each is a separate kingdom. Ireland is a great island. These countries are all in that part of the world called Europe.

FROM GRIPLA.

Bavaria is bounded by Saxony; Saxony is bounded by Holstein, and next is Denmark. The sea runs between the eastern countries. Sweden is east of Denmark. Norway is to the north; Finmark is east of Norway; from thence the land extends to the northeast and east, until you come to Biarmeland; this land is under tribute to Gardaridge. From Biarmeland lie desert places all northward to the land which is called Greenland, [which, however, the Greenlanders do not affirm, but believe to have seen it otherwise, both from drift timber, that is known and cut down by men, and also from reindeer which have marks upon their ears, or bands upon their horns, likewise from sheep which stray here, of which there are some remaining in Norway, for one head hangs in Throndheim, and another in Bergen, and many others are to be found.][1] But there are bays, and the land stretches out towards the southwest; there are ice mountains, and bays, and islands lie out in front of the ice mountains; one of the ice mountains cannot be explored, and the other is half a month's sail, to the third, a week's sail. This is nearest to the settlement called Hvidserk. Thence the land trends north; but he who desires to go by the settlement, steers to the southwest. Gardar, the bishop's seat, is at the bottom of Ericsfiord; there is a church consecrated to holy Nicholas. There are twelve churches in the eastern settlement, and four in the western.

---

[1] The part inclosed in brackets is an interpolation of a recent date, and without any authority.

Now it should be told what is opposite Greenland, out from the bay, which was before named. Furdustrandur[1] is the name of the land; the cold is so severe that it is not habitable, so far as is known. South from thence is Helluland, which is called Skrællings land. Thence it is not far to Vinland the Good, which some think goes out to Africa.[2] Between Vinland and Greenland, is Ginnungagah, which runs from the sea called *Mare Oceanum*, and surrounds the whole earth.

---

[1] Not to be confounded with the place of the same name at Cape Cod.

[2] This is another passage upon which Bancroft depends, to prove that the locality of Vinland was unknown, when in the Sagas the position is minutely described, the situation being as well known as that of Greenland.

INDEX.

Adalbrand, 104.
Adam of Bremen, xlix, *n*, 36.
Adzer, Archbishop, xxviii.
Ægisif, 107.
Ælian, xiii.
Africa, 107, 108, 110.
Agassiz, Prof., 30, *n*.
Alf. of Dolum, 88.
Alfarin Valeson, 12.
Alfonso, xxlvii.
Alps, 107.
Alteson, Jorund, 18.
America, iii.
Amund, Bishop, xxxiv.
Andreas, xxxiii.
Annales Flateyensis, 104, *n*.
Annales Islandorum Regii, 104, *n*.
Annales, Reseniini, 104, *n*.
Anson, Lord, xxxviii.
Antioch, 106, 107.
Antiquarians, Royal Society of, lv, *n*.
Antiquitates Americanæ, lvii, *n*.
Apulia, 107.
Archæologia, Americana, 88, *n*.
Archer, 29, *n*, 31, *n*, 66, *n*.
Argyle, Marquis of, liv, *n*.
Aristotle, xiii.
Arnæ, Magnæan Collection, 48.
Arnbiorn, 89, 94, 97.
Arnlaug, 17, 25.
Arnold, xxix, xxxii; Gov. Benedict, lviii, *n*.
Asbrand, 92; Biorn, of Kamb, 89.
Asia, 106; Minor, 106; Great, 106, 107.
Aslak, 19, 49.
Assonnet Neck, lv, *n*, lvii.
Athelstane, xxxvii.
Atlantis, xiii.
Atli the Red, 86, 88.
Avalldania, 63, 70.
Azore, Island, 87, *n*.

Babylon, 106; new, 107.
Bacolon, Islands of, 104, *n*.
Bakka, 94.
Balder, 55, *n*.
Ball's River, xxxvi.
Bancroft, 108, *n*, 110, *n ;* Mr. George, xliii ; his views controverted, xliii, liv, *n*.
Baptistery, lvii.
Bardarson, Ivan, 12, *n ;* see Ivar Bert.
Bartholomew, the Apostle, 106.
Beacon, Mr. Joseph, 44, *n*.
Beamish, iii, iv, xix, 104, *n*, 105, *n*.
Bear Island, 67.
Bede, the Venerable, xxiv, xxxiv, *n*.
Behring Straits.
Beresvig, Roin, 12.
Bergen, 109.
Berse, Haldor's son, 13.
Bert, Ivar, xxxi, 12, *n*.
Bessalangen, 105.
Bethencourts, xvi.
Biafal, 66 ; see Kiafal.
Biarne, Bishop, 71, 76, 82; Butter-Tub, 49, *n*, 51.
Biarney, Isle, 65.
Biorn, Asbrandson Breidaviking, lii, 9, 91, 92; exiled, 93; returns, 94, 95, 96 ; goes abroad, 100, 103.
Biorneland, 108, 109.
Blaaserk, 16, 19.
Blaland, 107.
Blig, Thord, 95, 96.
Blue Hills, 62, *n*.
Bogafiord, 17, 20.
Borgafiord, East, 105.
Borgafiorden, 13.
Bork, the Fat, 89.
Bougainville, xiv.
Bory, de St. Vincent, xvi.
Braaville, lvii, *n*.
Brage, 55, *n*.
Brattahlid, xxvi.
Bredobolstad, 19.
Breidafiord, 17, 20.
Breidavik, 89.
Brereton, 29, *n*.
Brokö, 19.
Broughton, xviii.
Brun, Malte, lix, *n*, lx, *n*.
Bulgaria, 107.
Bull, Papal, xxv, *n* 2.

112　INDEX.

Burislaus, 93, n.
Burnet, liv, n.
Burnt, Nial, 98, n.
Buynirlfson, Dr., xxxi.
Buzzard's Bay, 31, n.
Byrdusmior, Biarne, 49.
Byzantium, xxxvi.

Cabot, xxxviii, 105, n.
Cadiz, viii.
Canaria, xv.
Canary Islands, xiv, xv, xvi, xvii, n.
Canute, xxxvii.
Cape Cod, v, xlvii, 29, n ; old ship at, 30, n.
Cape Farewell, xxviii.
Cape Malabar, 31, n.
Capraria, xv, xvi.
Carl Muller, xiv.
Chaplains, xvii.
Chappell, 28, n.
Chatham, 30, n.
Chaucer, 98, n.
Chingwank, lv, n.
Christ, 55, 67.
Christophersen, Claudius, xxv, n 2.
Cinnamon, 36, n.
Clarendon, Lord, liv, n.
Cock Lane ghost, liii.
Codex Flatoiensis, xli.
Colæns, xiii.
Colonization of Greenland, 15; of Iceland, xxi.
Columbus, xlviii, liv. 24, n, 104, n.
Constantinople.
Crantor, xxii, 59, n, 61, n.
Crantz, xxxv.
Crete, 107.
Cronica General de Espana, xlvii.
Cross, worshiped, lx, n.
Crossness, 42.
Culdees, xxiv.
Cyprus, 107.

Dagmalstad, 33, n.
Danforth, Dr., lv, n.
Darien, Isthmus of, 86, n.
Dasent, xxxvi.
De Barros, xvii, n.
De Fries, Rev., xxx.
Denmark, 107, 109.
Dicuil, xxiv, n.
Dighton Rock, xxx, n, lv, lvi, lvii, n, 12, n.
Digramula.
Dimonsvaag, 19.
Disco, 32.
Dögardarness.
Donsk tunga, xx.
Drangey, 16, 19.

Drapstock, 21, 23.
Drift-wood, 14, n.
Druidism, xix, n.
Dublin, 64, 103.
Dudley, Lieut. Gov., 32, n.
Duneyjar, 104, n.

Earl Sigvald, 100.
Early Christianity in America, traces of, xviii; history of, xxvii, n. 2.
Earth, brief description of, 106.
East Indies, xlviii. n.
Easton, Peter, lviii, n.
Echard, liv, n.
Egede, Rev. Hans, xxxv, 61, n.
Egypt, 107.
Einar, 13, 17, 19, n, 25.
Eindridesuden, 105.
Elysium, xiii.
England, 106.
Enne, 12.
Ephesus, 106.
Eric, Bishop, lvii.
Eric, the Red, xxv, xxvi ; accepts Christianity,xxvii; goes to Greenland, li, 17, 19 ; resolves to seek new land, 12, 18; banished, 19 ; returns to Greenland, 20, 22 ; his accident, 28.
Erickső, 20 ; see Ericseya.
Ericseya, 16.
Ericsfiord, xxvi, 109.
Ericson, Thovald, xlvii, li ; goes to Vinland, 39 ; his death, 41, 62, 65 ; Thorstein, li, 22 ; sails for Vinland, 43 ; returns, 43 ; his death, 45.
Ericstad, 16.
Erie, Bishop Upse, liii, 104.
Erlandson, Hauk, xxiii, n, 11, n, 48.
Espihol, 76.
Esquimaux.
Ethelred, xxxvii.
Euphrates, 106.
Europe, 107, 109.
Eyktarstad, 32, 33, n.
Eyolfson, Bishop Magnus, xlviii, n.
Eyrbyggia Saga, 89.
Eyvind, 85.

Fall River, lix, n.
Farm, Leamington, lviii.
Faroese, Ballad of, xlix, n.
Feather Islands, 104.
Fenris, 55, n.
Fiedspidæ, 20.
Finboge, 77 ; sailed for Vinland, 77 ; murdered, 79.
Finn the Handsome, xlix, n.
Finnmark, 107, 109.

INDEX. 113

Flatö, island of, xli.
Florida, 87, *n*.
Flosè, 76.
Forsark, Thorkel, swims for a sheep, 26.
Forster, J. Reinhold, xlix.
Fortunate isles, xiv, xv.
Foster, Father, 34, *n*.
Fragments, geographical, 105.
France, 107.
Frederick, bishop, 17.
Frederikshab, xxviii.
Frey, 55, *n*.
Freydis, 51, 77, *n* ; sailed for Vinland, 77; quarrels with the company, 78; murders the brothers and their company; returns to Greenland, 80.
Fridgerda, 49.
Friederichstal, xxxi.
Frisland, 107.
Frithiof's Saga, xxiii, *n*, 52, *n*.
Froda, 91, 95.
Frode, Ari, xxiii, xxiv, *n*, xlvi.
Fuerteventura, xvi.
Furderstrand, 73; see Wonderstrand.
Furdustrandur, 110.

Galdrakin, Thorgrim, 96.
Games, 64.
Gamlason, Thorhall, 49.
Ganges, 106.
Gardar, xxi; location of, xxix, *n* ; cathedral of, xxx; marriage in, xxxiii, *n*, 77, 109.
Gardaridge, 109.
Gaspe, lix, *n*.
Geir, the Priest, 98.
Gellarson, Thorgeir, 16.
Geller, Thord, 49; Thorkel, 88.
Geon, 107.
Germany, 107.
Geyser, xxii.
Gilbert, 29, *n*, 3.
Gisli, the Outlaw, 18, *n*.
Gisser, 38.
Gissur, the White, xxxii, *n*.
Glamberland, 81.
Gnupson, Bishop Eric, xxviii.
Gode, 89, *n*.
Godthaab, xxviii.
Goe, Month of, 14.
Gomera, xvi.
Gornbornese-Skare, 12, *n* ; see Gunnbiorn's Rocks.
Gosnold, 29, *n*, 53, *n*.
Gottland, 108.
Gould, Sabine-Baring, xliv, *n*.
Graah, Captain, xxviii.

Grammaticus, Saxo, lvi, *n*.
Grapes, 54.
Graysteel, 19, *n*.
Great Ireland, 64, 86, 87, *n*.
Greece, 107.
Greenland, discovery of, xxv; progress of, xxvi; tributary to Norway, xxvii; church organized in, xxviii; monuments and ruins, xxx; explorations in, xxxii; trade of, xxxiii; last bishop of, xxxiii; decline of, xxxiii; lost Greenland found, xxxv; Queen Margaret prohibits trade, xxxv; ruins in, 21; cattle, 26; Christianity introduced, 108, 109.
Greenlander, Jon., xxxiv.
Gregory, iv, xxv, *n*, 2.
Grettir, Saga, xliv, *n*, 28, *n*.
Grimhild, her death, 44.
Grimkel, 12.
Grimolfson, Biarne, 49, 51; lost in the Worm Sea, 63, *n*.
Gripla, 106, 109.
Gudlaug the Rich, 100.
Gudlaugson, Gudleif, lii; goes to Dublin, 100; carried to sea, 101, 102.
Gudrid, 37, 44, 45; second marriage, 57, 72; goes to Vinland, 51, 64, 72; goes to Rome, 81, *n*; a nun, 8.
Gudrun, 76.
Gunnbiorn, xxv ; his rocks, li, 12, 11, 12, 13; money found at, 14.
Gunnstein, 13.
Gunthorm Stale, 105.

Hafgerdingar, 22, *n*, 25.
Hafrafell, 85.
Haki, 53, 66,
Haldor, xxxiii, 13.
Halifax, 29.
Halla, 76.
Hallbera, Fru, Abbess of Stad, 76.
Hallfrida, 71, 76, 82.
Halmond, xliv, *n*.
Halogaland, xxxviii.
Hanno, xiv.
Harald Harfagr, xxi.
Hardicanute, xxxvii.
Harold, The Stern, xxxvii.
Harvard college, lv, *n*.
Hauk, Herr, 76.
Haukdal, 16, 18, 19.
Havgrim, 17, 22.
Head brink, 94.
Head, Sir Edmund, xl, *n*, xlvi.
Heath, lix, *n*.
Hebrides, 25, 90.
Heimdal, 35, *n*.
Hekia, 53, 66.

Heimskringla, iii, 87, *n*, xxxvii, *n*, xlvii, lvi, *n*.
Hela, 55.
Helge, 77; sailed for Vinland, 77; murdered, 79; the Lean, 86.
Helgefell, 89, 91, 100.
Helluland, liii, 65, 108, 110.
Helsingeland, 108.
Henningson, Magnus, xxxv.
Heriulf, 21, 23, *n*, 25.
Heriulfness, xxiv.
Heriulfson, Biarne, li; goes to Norway, 27; goes to Greenland, 22; sees new land, 23, 24; settles, 25.
Herodotus, xlvii.
Hesperides, xv.
Hialte, xxvii, *n* 3, 38.
Hispania, 107.
Historic Genealogical Register, 30, *n*.
Historiske Mindesmærker, Grönland, 11, 15, 87, *n*.
Hitardale, 16.
Hoby, lvi, *n*.
Höfda-Strand, 49.
Högni the White, 85.
Holmgard, 107.
Holstein, 109.
Holsteinborg, xxviii.
Homer, xiii, xlvii.
Homstater, 20.
Honey Dew, 31, *n*.
Hop, 60, 70; see Mt. Hope.
Horse head, Thord, 49.
Hortado, Mary, 61, *n*.
Hreidarson, Ulf, 12.
Husasnotru, 81, *n*.
Hvalsö, 26.
Hvalsöfiord, 26.
Hvidserk, 109.
Hvitrammana-land, lii, 86.
Hymn to Thor, 55, 67.

Iceland, discovery, xxi; colonization, xxi; birds of, xxii; mammalia, xxii; Christianity introduced, xxxi, 17; date of manuscripts, xli; the Saga-men, xii; printing press established, xlvii; The Eddas, xlvii.
Icelandic, grammat. structure of, iv.
Iduna, 55, *n*.
Igaliko, xxx, lvi.
Illuge, 19.
India, 106.
Indialand, 106.
Indians, Gaspe, lix, *n*.
Ingigerd, 76.
Ingolf, xxii, 21, 25, 53, *n*.
Ingolfshodi, xxii, *n*, xxiii.
Iona, Isles of, xxiv.

Ireland, 108, 109.
Ireland the Great, xviii.
Irish Monks, xxi, *n*; books of, xxiii; bells and croziers of, xxiv, 101.
Ironsides, Biarne, 49.
Irving, Washington, xliv, xlviii, *n*.
Islands, Greek, 107.
Isle, of Currents, 54; Nauset, 29, *n*, 31, *n*, 53, 66; of Sable, 52, *n*.
Isles, of America, xviii; of the Blessed, xiv.
Italy, lvii, 107.

Jardar, xxv, 12, *n*, 15.
Jerusalem, 106.
John, the Apostle, 106.
Johnson, Biorn, 48; Dr., liii.
Joinville, xlvii.
Jomsberg, Vikings, 93.
Jones, Inigo, lix, *n*.
Jord, the Earth, 91, *n*.
Jorund, 16, 76, 88.
Julian's Hope, xxviii, xxx.
Juno, Temple of, xvi.
Junonia, xv, xvi, xvii.

Kakortok, xxx.
Kalbrunarskald, Thormod, 13.
Kallstegg, xxiii, *n*; iv, *n*.
Kamb, 97.
Kanitsok, lvii.
Karkortok, lvii.
Karlsefne, lix; Thorfinn, lii, lvi, *n*, 3, *n*; goes to Greenland, 49; marriage, 51, 72; sails for Vinland, 51, 64, 72; sails past Wonder-strand, 55; trades, 58, 73; battle with natives, 59, 75; seeks Thorhall, 61; sails south, 55; kills some Skrællings, 60; returns to Greenland, 63, 75, 177; goes to Iceland, 71, 76; goes to Norway, 80; cuts wood, 108; Snorre, born, 74, 76, 82.
Kendal, A. E., lvii, *n*.
Ketil, 17, 25, 89.
Kiafal, 53.
Kialarness, 40, 52, 65.
Kiarten, 93, 95, 103.
King, Christian II, xxxv; Christian III, xxxv; Frederic II, xxxv; Henry of Portugal, xvii, *n*; Harold, xxiv, xlv, 93; Juba II, xv, xvi; Magnus, xxxii; Olaf the Saint, 100; Olaf Tryggvesson, Saga of, xxxviii, 18; accepts Christianity, xxvi; his swimming match, xxxvii; ship of, xxxviii; Sweno, xlix, *n*; Nebuchadnezzar, 106.

INDEX. 115

Kingiktorsoak, xxxi.
Kingsborough, xvii.
Kittlebiarne, 38, *n*.
Knarrabringa, Thorbiary, 16, 18, 88.
Kodranson, Thorvold, 17.
Kol, 18, *n*.
Kolgrimsson, Hroar, xxx.
Kruge, Ulf, 113.
Krok, Thorvald, 76.
Kroksfiardarheidi, xxxii.
Kvendland, 108.

Labrador, 28, *n*.
Laing, iii, iv, lvii, *n*; Prof., xxxix.
Lake, 69; houses built at, 70.
Lancerote, xvi.
Landa-Rolf, 105.
Landnama Book, xxiii, *n* 1, 11.
Law of matrimony, 79, *n*.
Leamington, lviii, *n*.
Leclerc, Father, lix.
Ledchammar, xxxviii.
Leif, xxvi, li, lii, 18, 22, 26; goes to Vinland, 27; returns to Greenland, 36; finds shipwrecked sailors, 36, 38, 39; sent to proclaim Christianity in Greenland, 38, 39; his Booths, lix, 40, 50, 72, 105, *n*; his judgment on Freydis, 80, 88; the Lucky, 108.
Leikskaale, 19.
Literature of Iceland, xliii; Anglo-Saxon, xlvi; of France, xlvii; Castilian, xlvii.
Lizards, xvii.
Lodbrok, Rognar, 49.
Logman's Annall, 104, *n*.
Löigardelen, 13.
Loke, 55, *n*.
Lombardland, 107.
Lombardy, 107.
Long Serpent, xxxviii.
Loptson, Thorolf Eyar, 100.

Machin, Robert, xvii, *n*.
Madeira, xvi.
Madr, lvi, *n*.
Magnus, Olaus, xl.
Magnussen, Prof., Finn, xxxi, xxxiii, xlvii, 77, 27, *n*.
Magre, Haldor, 105.
Maine, liv, *n*.
Major, xvi.
Malte Brun, 32, *n*.
Man, Isle of, 90.
Manamoyake Bay, 31, *n*.
Manuscripts, date of, xli.
Manvel, Juan, xlvii.
Mar, 86, 99.

Marana, John Paul, xix.
Markland, liii, 29, *n*, 65, 105, 108.
Mars, Vigdis, xxx.
Marson, Are, lii, 85, 86, *n*, 87, *n*, 88, *n*.
Martha's Vineyard, 54, *n*.
Massachusetts, 108, *n*.
Massur Wood, 81.
Mather, Dr. Cotton, lv, *n*, 46, *n*; his *Magnalia*, 46, *n*, 58, *n*, 61, *n*, 74, *n*.
Mathieson, xxx.
Mauritania, xx.
Medafeels-strand, 90.
Mediterranean, 106, 107.
Merry Mount, 32, *n*.
Mexico, British Language in, xix.
Midgard, 35, *n*.
Midjokul, 16, 20.
Miklagard, 107.
Milesieus, xix, *n*.
Mill, Newport, lviii, *n*, Chesterton, lix, *n*.
Minor Narratives, lii, 86.
Missionaries, French, lix, *n*.
Mjorfiord, 13.
Money found, li.
Monuments, absence of, lv.
Moore, xix.
Morton, New English Canaan, 32, *n*.
Mossfell, 38, *n*.
Mount Desert, liv, *n*.
Mount Hope Bay, lii, 32, 56.
Mundia, 107.

Nadodd, xxi.
Narragansett Bay, 6, *n*.
Narratives, 1; their truthfulness, liii; their age, liv; Major Narratives, 9; Minor, 83.
Nantucket, 30, *n*, 32, *n*.
Neprass, Hergill, 87.
Ness Röin, 12.
Newfoundland, liii.
Newport, lviii, *n*, lix, *n*.
Niall, xix.
Nicholas, 109.
Nidaros, 18.
Nile, 107.
Nineveh, 106.
Nivaria, xv.
Nordenfield, 95.
Nordrsetur, xxxii.
North American Review, iii.
Northern Antiquarians, xlix, 29, *n*.
Northmen, xviii, xx; character and achievements of, xxxvi; ships of, xxxvii; colonize Greenland, xxxvii; discover America, xxxvi; nautical knowledge of, xl.

Northumbria, xxxvii.
Norway, 107, 109.
Nutmegs, 36, n.
Nyja, 105, n.
Nyja Land, 104, n.
Nyjafundu-land, 105, n.

Ocean, Pacific, 108.
Oceanum, Mare, 110.
Oddson, Eindrid, xxxi.
Odin, xxii, n, xxii, 9, n, 55, v, n.
Ocland, 108.
Ogursvigen, 13.
O'Halloran, xix.
Olaf, the Saint, xxxvii.
Old Mill, lviii, n.
Ombrios, xv, xvi.
Orcobares, 106.
Ord, 91, 82.
Orkneys, 90.
Ormuzd, xxii.
Orne, the Lean, 89.
Otis, Amos, 30, n.

Paley, Dr., liv.
Palfrey, lix, n.
Palingenesia, xxii.
Palma, xvi.
Palnatoki, 93, n, 94.
Palteskia, 107.
Papey, Island of, xxiv.
Papyli, Island of, xxiv.
Paradise, 106, 107.
Parentals, 92.
Parry, xxxi.
Peak of Teneriffe.
Pelham, Edward, lviii, n.
Penguin Islands, 104, n.
Penobscot, i, iv, n.
Peringskiold, 32, n, 36, n, 40, n.
Permia, 108, 109.
Peter, the Apostle, 106.
Peyrere, xxv, n 2, xxxiv.
Pharaoh Necho, xiv.
Phenicians, xiii, xiv, xvii.
Phœnius, xix, n.
Pillars of Hercules, xii, xiii.
Pison, 106.
Plato, xiii.
Pliny, xv, xvi, 57.
Pluviala, xvi.
Plutarch, xvi.
Plymouth Colonists, xlvii.
Point Alderton, 40, n.
Point Care, 66.
Point Gilbert, 30, n, 31, n, 40, n, 53, n, 66, n.
Popham, George, 36, n.
Port Haldiman, 29.
Priests of Sais, xiii.

Prince Henry the Navigator, xvi, 72, n.
Prince Madoc, xx.
Purchas, His Pilgrimage, 12, n.
Puerto Bello, 63, n.
Purpurariæ, xv, xvi.
Pulsland, 107.

Queen Margaret, xxxv.

Race Point, 40, n.
Rafn, Holm-Gang, 16, 19; Prof., iv, v; the Limerick merchant, 85, 86, 88, xviii, xxxiii, xlix; his Antiquities of America, xlix, lv, lvi, 15, 25, 30, n, 31, n, 87, n, 103.
Rask, Professor, xxxi.
Raudulf, xxxviii.
Rauglatr, 76.
Red-beard, 67; see Thor.
Reikiavik, xxiii, 12, 76.
Rhine, 107.
Rhode Island, li; Historical Society of, lvi.
Robertson, Rev. Dr., xlix.
Rocks, Portsmouth, lvii, n; Tiverton, lvii, n.
Rofnsgripa, 17.
Roger Guiscard, xxxvi, n.
Rolf of Rödesand, 13, 104.
Rollo, xxxvii.
Rönhavnos, 94, 100.
Round Towers, lix, n.
Runamoc, lvi, n.
Runic Letters, on an oar, xxxiv; age of Alphabet, xviii; in Grettir Saga, xliv, n.
Runolfson, Bishop Thorlak, 71, 76, 82.
Russia, 107, 108.

Sacred Fish, 57, 69.
Sæmund the Wise, xlvi.
Sagadahoc, 36, n.
Sagas, iii, iv, 110, n; general knowledge of, xlix.
St. Columba, xviii; Paul, liv; Patrick, xviii; John, lii; Savior, liv, n.
St. Sophia, 107.
Salmon, 32.
Saxavol, 12.
Saxe, son of Alfarin Valeson, 15.
Saxo Grammaticus, xlviii.
Saxon, v.
Schöning, 87, n.
Schoolcraft, Henry, lv, n.
Scotland, 108.
Scots, 53.
Sea of Darkness, xii.

INDEX.   117

Seat, Episcopal, 106; of Gardar, 108, 109.
Seat Posts, 19; see Setstakkar.
Serkland, 107.
Sertorius, xiv.
Setstakkar, xxii, n.
Shawanese Indians, 87, n.
Sicily, 107.
Sida, 105.
Sighvatson, Erling, xxxi.
Sigurd, Earl of the Orkneys, 90.
Skagafiord, 81.
Skalholt, xxxi, v.
Skardfa, Binéren von, xxxiv.
Skeleton in armor, lix, n.
Skialdespilder, Eyvind, xlv.
Skötufiorden, 13.
Skrællings, xxxii, xxxiii, 21, 41, 57; Trade with Karlsefne, 58, 69, 70, 73; one killed 74.
Skrællings land, 110.
Slaves, 18, n, 19, 53.
Sledges, 98.
Slut Bush, 30, n.
Smællingar, 41, n.
Smalenskia, 107.
Smith, Capt. John, 29, n; Joshua Toulmin, iii, iv; Mr. Philip, 46, n.
Smith's Dialogues, 42.
Snæbiorn, Galte, 13; killed 14, 15, n.
Snæfell, mountain of, xxxii.
Snœfellsjokull, 16.
Snorre, 89, 91, 93, 96, 97, 98, 99, 102.
Snow, 70.
Snowland, xxi.
Soers, Eyulf, 16.
Sokke, xxix.
Solon, xiii.
Solvi, 17, 25.
Sondensfield, 95.
Spainland, 107.
Speculum Regali, xl.
Stærbiorn, 13.
Stafholt, 13.
Statius Sebosus, xv, xvi.
Steinum, 76.
Sterka, Herr Ereland, 76.
Stilicho, xix, n, 1.
Strabo, xix, xvii.
Straum Bay, 54, 70; see Stream Bay.
Straumey, 66.
Styrbiorn, 93, 94, n, 97.
Straumfiord, 100.
Stream Bay, 54.
Stuf, the Skald, xlv.
Sturlingers, 100.
Styrmer, xxiii, n, 11, n.
Sukkeroppen, xxviii.
Sumarlide, 13.

Superstition, 28, n.
Sweden, 107; the lesser, 108.
Swein, xxxvii.
Sydero, 19.

Tacenta, 86, n.
Tacitus, xix, n, 2.
Taunton, lv, n.
Thor, xxii, n, xxiv, 9, n, 35, n, 54, 55.
Thorberg, xxxviii, n.
Thorbiorg, 86.
Thorbiorn, 65; the Fat, 89, 91; Vifilson, 16.
Thorbjornglora, 17, 25.
Thorbrandson, Helgi, 17, 25; Snowe, 49.
Thord, 49, 72.
Thordarson, Biorn, xxxi; Snorre, 72.
Thordsen, xxiii, n, 11, n.
Thordis, 76.
Thorer the Idle, 39.
Thorfinn, Earl of the Orkneys, 88.
Thorgeir, 71, 76; Red, 13.
Thorgest, 16, 19, 20.
Thorgills, Kollson, 88.
Thorgird, 21.
Thorgrim, Styr, 16.
Thorhall the Hunter, 51, 54, 65, 67, 68.
Thorhild, xxvii, 16; her church, 47; the Partridge, 49.
Thorkafiord, 85.
Thorkatla, 87.
Thorkel, 13, 14.
Thorlacius, Bishop, 32, n.
Thorod, 13, killed, 14, 15, n.
Thorodd, 90, 91, 92, 93, 95, 96, 97, 100; Wooden Clog, 91.
Thoruna, 49.
Thorsnesthing, 93.
Thorstein Black, 44, 82, n.
Thoruna, 71, 76, 82.
Thorvald, son of Helge, 104; son of Osvald, 15, 16.
Thorvord, 52.
Theopompus, xii.
Thingness, 13, 14.
Throndheim, 18, 109.
Thurid, 51, n, 76; of Froda, 89, 91, 102, 103.
Tigris, 106.
Timber cut, 73.
Todum, 19.
Torfæus, xxxi; works of, xlix, 32, n, 48.
Tradition, Indian, lvii, n.
Traditions, xviii.
Turkish Spy, xix.
Tyrians, xiii.
Tyrker, 28, 34, 35.

Ulf Krage, xxv, 16.
Ulf Oexna-Thorerisson, 15.
Ulf the Squinter, 85, 88.
Unipeds, 61.
Uvæge, 63, 70.

Vag, 21.
Val, 91, 92.
Valldidia, 63, 70.
Valgerda, 76.
Valthiof, 18.
Vathelldi, 63, 70.
Vatnahver, 17, 18, 25.
Vatshorn, 16.
Vermeland, 108.
Villehardouin, xlvii.
Vinland, xxvii, n 1, lvii, 108; Bancroft's Views of, xliii, n; known by Adam of Bremen, xlix, n, 36, n; known by the Irish, xlix, n, liii, lvi; climate, 32, 67; situation of, 87; the Good, 108, 110.
Vivien de St. Martin, xiv.
Voyages — Eric the Red, 15–21; Biarne, 21–26; Leif's, 26–43; Thorstein's, 43–48; Karlsefne's, 48–76; Freydis, 77–82; Helge, 77–

Voyages, continued —
82; Finboge, 77–82; Marson's, 85–88; Asbrandson's, 89–100; Gudlangson's, 100–13; Miscellaneous, 103–105; Phenicians, xiv.

Wafer, 8, 6, n.
Waldemar the Great, 93, n.
Walkendorf, Archbishop Eric, xxxv.
Wallin, 93, n.
Warwick, lix, n.
Warwickshire, lviii, n, lix, n.
Webb, Dr., 31, n.
Werlauf, 14, n.
Whales, 54, 56, 73.
Wheat, 54, 66.
White-man's land, 63, 70, 86, 87, n, 88.
Winthrop, Prof., lv, n.
Wonder-strand, 30, n, 53, n, 66, n, 69.
Woodland, 105, n.
Woodrow, liv, n.
Wormius, xxxiv.
Worm Sea, 63, 70.
Writing Rock; see Dighton Rock.

Yule, 50.

www.ingramcontent.com/pod-product-compliance
Lightning Source LLC
Chambersburg PA
CBHW022114160426
43197CB00009B/1021